W. Kirk MacNulty

FREEMASONRY

Symbols, Secrets, Significance

With 386 illustrations, 327 in color

Thames & Hudson

To my wife, Christine

p. 1: An early 19th-century papier mâché box, possibly showing Scottish Rite symbols.
p. 2: An 18th-century floor cloth, used in ritual.
p. 3: A 19th-century Dutch apron, showing the Square and Compasses.
This spread: The raising ceremony of the Third Degree in an 18th-century French print.

© 2006 Thames & Hudson Ltd, London

First published in 2006 in hardcover in the United States of America by Thames & Hudson Inc., 500 Fifth Avenue, New York, New York 10110

thamesandhudsonusa.com

Library of Congress Catalog Card Number
2005911290

ISBN-13: 978-0-500-51302-6
ISBN-10: 0-500-51302-3

Printed and bound in Singapore by C.S. Graphics

FREEMASONRY

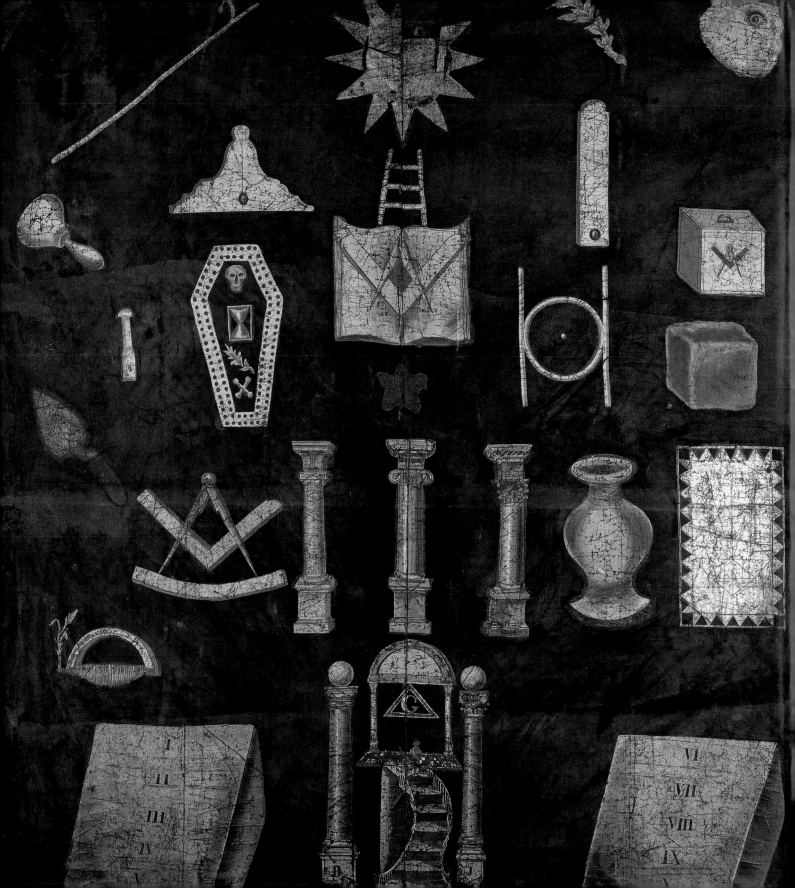

CONTENTS

INTRODUCTION

A book about Freemasonry, particularly one written to include readers who are not Masons, should certainly start with some information about the nature and history of the Masonic Order. A definition of the Order is relatively easy: Freemasonry is a secular fraternal organization, traditionally open only to men. It promulgates the principles of morality and seeks to advance the practice of brotherly love and charitable action among all persons – not simply among Masons. It is not a religion; but it is a society of religious men in the sense that it requires its members to believe in the existence of a 'Supreme Being'. The name of that Being, the scripture in which It is revealed, and the form in which It is to be worshipped is entirely the business of the individual Mason. When entering the Order, Masons take obligations on the 'Volume of Sacred Law', and each Mason takes his obligation on that particular volume of writings which *he* holds to be sacred. While encouraging each Brother to follow the teachings of his own religion, Freemasonry is not concerned with the detail of those religions; and sectarian religious discussion is forbidden at Masonic gatherings. While not a religion, the Order might be considered to be a 'philosophical companion to religion'. That idea is implicit in the definition, taken from the Lecture of the First Degree (Emulation Working), of Masonry as 'a peculiar system of morality, veiled in allegory and illustrated by symbols'.

Freemasonry's mode of operation is unusual. It communicates its teachings through a series of ritual dramas called 'Degrees' and by the use of an elaborate structure of symbols derived largely from the tools and practices of the stonemason's craft. The Degrees are conferred in a 'Masonic Lodge' which may be referred to as a 'Blue', 'Symbolic', 'Craft', or 'Private' Lodge. The Lodge is the basic unit of Masonic organization, and serves a local area. Depending upon the location, it may have a membership from about twenty to two hundred members. Each Private Lodge is responsible to a 'Grand Lodge' which is the official governing body in Freemasonry. Generally speaking, there is a Grand Lodge in each country;

Freemasonry can seem opaque to the uninitiated with its esoteric symbols that cover Masonic objects (as on the apron opposite), the peculiar regalia, and the solemn ritual (as depicted above in an 18th-century French print). However, for the Freemason who has experienced the rituals and lectures that form the basis of Freemasonry, everything has profound moral meaning.

Masonic Lodges can be formed around any number of shared common interests, and every Lodge has its own character. This page shows jewels for Lodges formed at work (above, the Lutine Lodge at Lloyds of London); by actors (above, middle, the Yorick Lodge); around a particular saint (above right, St Michael's Lodge); in the army (far right, London Scottish Rifles Lodge); and among alumni of a particular school (right, Old Cheltonian Lodge).

Opposite is an impressive Lodge room, lit to simulate sunrise in the East and sunset in the West. Such unique Lodge rooms may create a particular atmosphere, but few Lodges have their own rooms, and many meet in Masonic Centres, which serve several Lodges.

in the United States there is a Grand Lodge in each state. As mentioned, it is the purpose of a Masonic Lodge to confer the Three Degrees of Masonry, sometimes called the 'Craft Degrees'. These are the Entered Apprentice Degree, the Fellow Craft Degree, and the Master Mason Degree. The rituals relate to practices and events that were said to have occurred at the building of King Solomon's Temple. By participating in those Degrees the Candidate in the Craft Lodge is taught many things; but most importantly, the fundamental moral principles of Brotherly Love, Relief, and Truth. In one form or another, these principles are universal throughout all Masonic teachings. The ritual of each Degree is followed by an illustrated lecture that summarizes the drama and outlines the points which are taught by each of the events within the ritual. Some Lodges use contemporary audio-visual techniques to support these lectures, but many Lodges, those with a traditional orientation, use 'tracing boards'.

While the Craft Degrees communicate all the essential teachings of Freemasonry, during the many years of Masonry's history various Orders have evolved that confer 'Higher Degrees', open only to Master Masons (see a full discussion on pp. 181–213). These include the York Rite, Mark Masonry, the Scottish Rite, the Knights Templar, and the Shrine, to name just a few. These Higher Degrees, each of which has its own rituals and symbolism, do not impart additional knowledge; rather, they simply provide different emphasis and more detailed information about various aspects of the material in the first Three Degrees. Thus, it is frequently heard that while a Freemason may go on to attain many more degrees, his most important rank is that of a Master Mason.

The nature of the Masonic Degrees is not made available to the general public, and this has resulted in serious misunderstandings. An on-going fascination of some non-Masons with Freemasonry derives from the common misconception that it is a 'secret society'. This has caused many to assume

Some Lodges go beyond the standard Masonic regalia to add to the experience and sense of belonging, such as this Scottish Rite 'Anglo-Saxon Lodge'. The Master, centre, is dressed as King Solomon, who also appears in the plate above, with the architect of Solomon's Temple, Hiram Abiff, who is explaining his plans to the King. This story is at the root of Freemasonry.

Freemasonry communicates its teachings in many ways, but traditionally tracing boards are used. The term 'tracing board' recalls the boards inscribed with designs used by stonemasons to cut the stone to the correct shape and size; however, those used in Freemasonry are in fact collections of symbols organized in specific hierarchies. Many of these objects are brightly coloured and works of art in their own right. Here we see the basics of Masonic symbolism — the Chequered Pavement, symbol of good and evil in life; the two columns, derived from Solomon's Temple, that support celestial and terrestrial spheres; the Square and Compasses, which indicate a correctly lived life; and the Sun and Moon, symbols of duality.

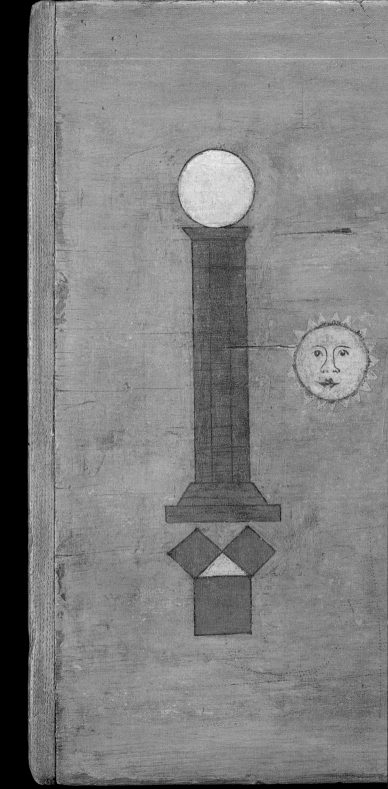

that Freemasons are involved in such things as worshipping Satan, planning to overthrow the government, or seeking in some way to manipulate society. None of these things is true; and although there is not much about Freemasonry in the news these days (the Order is not generally considered to be newsworthy unless it is alleged to be involved in some criminal activity) Freemasonry is actually a very public organization. Its buildings are prominent and plainly marked; it operates many charities (the beneficiaries of which are often not Masons); and Freemasons themselves are not in any way prohibited from making their membership known in public.

However, it is true that Masonic Lodges do conduct their meetings in private and that Masons are obligated not to divulge the secrets of the Order. These secrets have been defined by the United Grand Lodge of England as the means by which Freemasons identify themselves to each other; but, in fact, not even that is secret. Freemasonry has been abundantly supplied with apostates, and there are publications available at public libraries and on the Internet that reveal all the material which a Mason promises to hold close. Since this is the case, one might reasonably ask why Freemasonry continues to open itself to criticism by requiring its obligations of secrecy. The answer to this question is to be found in the teachings of the Order. Masonic secrecy is a symbol; and like all of the other Masonic symbols, it provides instruction. As some of the material in the following pages will indicate, if a Mason pursues his studies with serious commitment, he will learn remarkable things about himself. Profoundly personal material of this nature should not be shared with those who cannot understand it. It should be shared only with those who have had similar experience.

Even leaving the issue of secrecy aside, the structure of Freemasonry is undeniably complex to the outsider. This is exacerbated by the fact that since the beginning of formal Freemasonry in England in the early 18th century, various Grand Lodges have developed different ideas about the purposes of the Order and the activities appropriate for its members. The result is that today in some countries there is more than one Grand Lodge. Many of these competing Grand Lodges regard themselves as 'regular' and refer to their

Freemasons have often been accused of bizarre practices, and over the years there have been many exposés. The illustration above comes from the famous hoax by Léo Taxil, which purported to show what went on in Lodges, but was pure fiction. However, apart from when it is working in Lodge, it is an open organization – see for example, the very public display by Freemasons, opposite. The tower in the background belongs to the George Washington Masonic National Memorial, a public landmark in Virginia, United States.

KEEP WITHIN COMPASS.

BE SURE · TO AVOID MANY TROUBLES WHICH OTHERS ENDURE · KEEP WITHIN COMPASS · AND YOU SHALL

FEAR GOD

INDUSTRY

PRODUCETH WEALTH

Printed for & Sold by Carington Bowles,

Published as the Act directs 1 Nov 1785.

Nº 69 St Pauls Church Yard, London.

By honest and industrious means / Youll live at ease.

Then let the Compass be your guide, / And go where'er you please.

'Keep within Compass and you shall be sure / to avoid many troubles that others endure'.
uch messages are common in Freemasonry, which above all can be seen as a moral system.
Many of their phrases for upright living have crept into everyday speech — for example, the
hrases 'on the square', 'on the level' and 'straight talking'. Other Masonic phrases that hav
nfiltrated everyday language are 'Past Master' (denoting a particular competence) and 'to b
iven the Third Degree' (to be interrogated).

KEEP WITHIN COMPASS.

BE SURE . TO AVOID MANY TROUBLES WHICH OTHERS ENDURE. KEEP WITHIN COMPASS. AND YOU SHALL

FEAR GOD

PRUDENCE

PRODUCETH ESTEEM

Printed for & Sold by Carington Bowles,   Nº 69 Sᵗ Paul's Church Yard, London.

Published as the Act directs 9 Novʳ 1786.

Attend unto this simple fact,   *That virtuous and prudent ways,*
As thro' this life you rove.   *Will gain esteem and love.*

counterpart as 'irregular'. This situation has come about in large part due to the fact that there is no single international authority for Craft Freemasonry. Rather, the Grand Lodges that comply with a common set of principles 'recognize' each other as being 'regular'. Nevertheless, while there are some very important and deep-rooted reasons for these fundamental differences, which are discussed towards the end of this Introduction, the symbols associated with each of the Degrees do not vary substantially from jurisdiction to jurisdiction.

To understand Freemasonry completely, one must look to the history of the Order, and in particular to the various philosophies and traditions from which it was derived. Sadly, there is very little reliable information available. Some of the early Masonic histories written in the 18th and 19th centuries were quite fanciful and uncritical in their approach. Most of these writings associate the start of Freemasonry with the Biblical and Classical periods, and they imply a secret Order that operated through the medieval period and the Renaissance before finally becoming public in the early 18th century. More recent authors may have sought to be more rigorous, but writing on the subject of Freemasonry's origins in *The Art of Memory*, Frances A. Yates remarked that even more exacting researchers 'have to leave as an unsolved question the problem of the origin of "speculative" masonry, with its symbolic use of columns, arches, and other architectural features, and of geometrical symbolism, as the framework within which it presents a moral teaching and a mystical outlook towards the divine architect of the universe'. Thus, imaginative historical writings still persist. Recently, some authors have suggested that Freemasonry was started by Knights Templar who fled to Scotland to avoid persecution in France (though this idea has been discredited). Perhaps the best historical insight available can be obtained by looking at early members of the Order.

The first 'Freemasonic activity' we can observe with certainty occurs in England in the middle of the 17th century. The first speculative Masons that we can identify positively and about whom we have substantial information are Sir Robert Moray and Elias Ashmole. They were initiated in 1641 and 1646 respectively, both in the north of England. Moray appears to have been

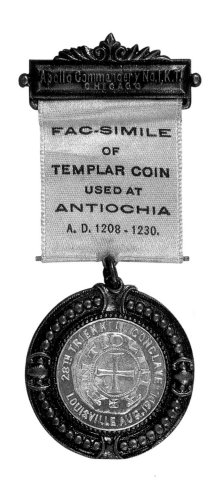

The jewel above, belonging to the Masonic Knights Templar Order, clearly wants to forge a link with the chivalric Orders of the past by referencing the original Knights Templar. Such continuity, however, is highly unlikely. In fact, much of the symbolism in Freemasonry comes from medieval stonemasonry, as can be seen in the tracing board opposite: the Square, the Level and the Plumb. In Freemasonry each of these is ascribed a particular moral quality, as well as functioning as badges of Office within the Lodge.

Elias Ashmole (1617–92) was one of the very earliest Freemasons. Fascinated by alchemy and the Hermetic tradition, he would have been familiar with the Rosicrucian texts of the early 17th century, and published a paper supporting that Order and its teachings. The remarkable image opposite is taken from a late 18th-century German Masonic publication on Rosicrucian diagrams – clearly the early Freemasons saw themselves as part of the same tradition.

initiated in a Scottish operative Lodge that was working with Scottish military forces in England; Ashmole was initiated in a 'casual Lodge' in Warrington, Lancashire. The names of the Brethren present at his initiation are recorded in Ashmole's diary, and that 'casual Lodge' appears to have contained no operative masons. We do not have a great deal of information on this subject, but we can say that in the north of England during the mid-to-late 17th century, groups of Masons met as 'casual Lodges', apparently for the purpose of 'making Masons'. Although we have virtually no records of these 'casual Lodges', we can assume that they continued to meet throughout the latter part of the 17th century. We can make this assumption because, although there was no formal organization, Freemasonry was starting to be of interest to the public, and various writings of the period speak of the Order. For example, Dr Robert Plot's *Natural History of Staffordshire* (*c.* 1684) outlines Masonic practices and tells us that 'persons of the most eminent quality did not distain to be of this Fellowship'.

The intellectual orientation of Ashmole and Moray provides interesting and useful information about the nature of early Freemasonry. Both men were founder members of the Royal Society of London which indicates that they were well-respected intellectuals. It is also significant that both were closely involved with the 'Hermetic/Cabbalistic tradition' as it has been defined by Frances A. Yates, and as discussed in the first section of this book. Elias Ashmole with his publication *Theatrum Chemicum Britannicum*, a catalogue of British alchemical works, was a significant contributor to the literature of that tradition; and Robert Moray was the patron of the alchemist Thomas Vaughan. From their involvement with the Hermetic/Cabbalistic tradition we can safely assume that both men had a mystical turn of mind. But why would Ashmole and Moray want to join a Masonic lodge? Apparently, during the late 16th and 17th centuries there seems to have been a practice among some Gentlemen in Scotland to join operative Masonic Lodges. Their reason for joining seems to have been the reputation that operative masons enjoyed during the Renaissance. The design and construction of large buildings such as cathedrals, castles, stately homes and fortifications required a substantial knowledge of many technical areas. Because of this,

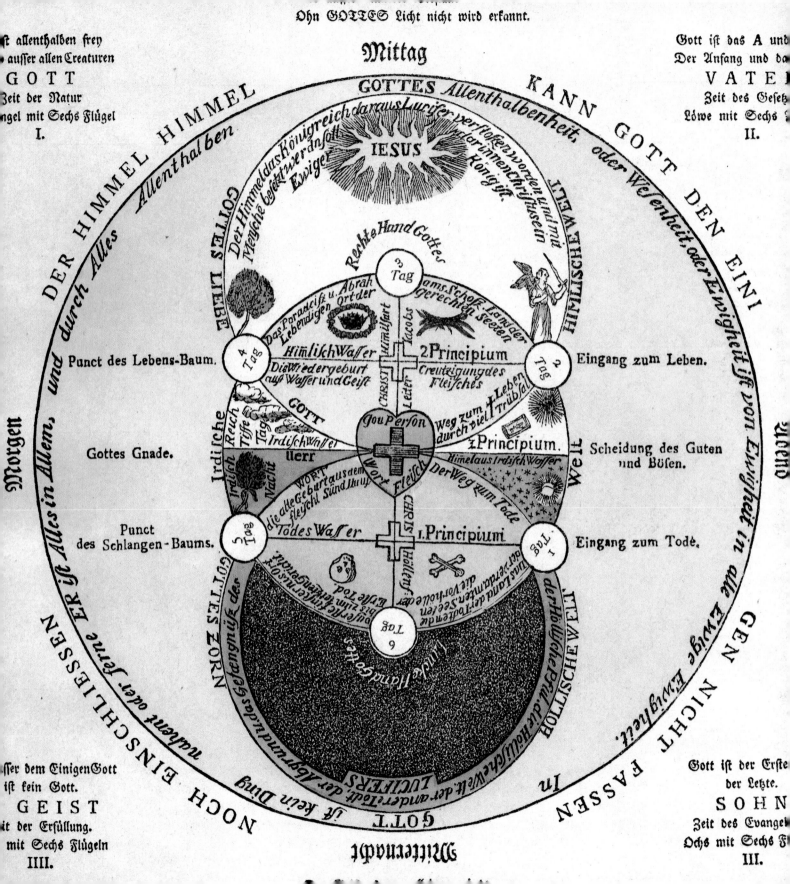

operative masons, particularly those of senior rank who participated in the design and supervision of this work as well as in the construction of the building itself, were well respected for their skills and knowledge of the Seven Liberal Arts and Sciences. Since the Seven Liberal Arts and Sciences were the framework of learning in the period, joining such a group provided a Gentleman with a substantial opportunity for education.

Leaving the historical uncertainties of origin behind, let us move on to some material of which we can speak confidently. On St John the Baptist's Day in 1717 four Masonic Lodges which are said to have been meeting 'from time immemorial', met at the Goose and Gridiron ale house in St Paul's Churchyard, London and constituted the first Grand Lodge. Anthony Sayer, Gentleman, was elected the Grand Master. This act brought into being the first public and formally acknowledged organization of Freemasons, and at the time it represented only Lodges in London. With the formation of this premier Grand Lodge Freemasonry expanded very quickly in terms of the influence of its membership. By 1721 the Duke of Montagu was the Grand Master. In 1723, six years after the foundation of the Grand Lodge, Dr James Anderson, a Scottish Presbyterian Minister residing in London at the time, published *The Constitutions of Freemasonry*. In the preparation of his *Constitutions*, Anderson is said to have consulted the opinions of 'the late and present Deputy Grand Masters and other learned Brethren'; and the work was published with a certain degree of Grand Lodge approval. Anderson's *Constitutions* formalized many useful and previously existing regulations, such as those prohibiting the discussion of politics and sectarian religious topics. It also sets out Masonry's requirement for the belief in a Supreme Being.

With the founding of the premier Grand Lodge in 1717, Freemasonry grew explosively. By 1730 the number of Private Lodges had grown from four to over seventy, and the area governed by the Grand Lodge had expanded to include provinces throughout England. The Grand Lodge was also granting authority to constitute Lodges abroad, the first ones being in Spain (Gibraltar) and India. In 1737 the initiation of Frederick Lewis, Prince of Wales created the first English Royal Freemason; and in doing so established an association between the British Royal Family and Freemasonry

Early Freemasonry based its authority on a collection of manuscripts known together as the 'Old Charges' – the one above, the Lechmere Manuscript, dates to c. 1670; the oldest, the Regius Manuscript, dates to c. 1390. The various regulations in these 'Old Charges' were written for operative craftsmen. The first regulations for Freemasonry as it is known today were Anderson's Constitutions *of 1723. Like the 'Old Charges' it also contained an imaginary history of the Order.* Constitutions *have been republished with modifications periodically – opposite, in the frontispiece to the 1784 Book of Constitutions,* Truth *illuminates the Lodge Hall.*

Below is a stunning brooch made by French prisoners-of-war held in England in the early 19th century. The time and effort that went into the work speaks volumes of the Freemason's dedication to his Craft.

which continues today. The formation of the premier Grand Lodge formalized Masonry throughout the British Isles. In Ireland speculative Lodges seem to have formed directly and very quickly. The Grand Lodge of Ireland was formed in 1730 and the Grand Lodge of Scotland in 1736. In 1751 a second Grand Lodge was organized in London. It called itself the Antient Grand Lodge, and was to compete with the premier Grand Lodge for over sixty years. This rivalry was resolved by the formation of the United Grand Lodge of England, and in due course we will consider that process in detail.

The establishment of the first formal Masonic organization in London in 1717 also had significant effects outside of Britain. During the period from 1717 to 1740 Masonic Lodges were formed throughout Northern Europe. The first French lodge, the Loge Au Louis d'Argent, was formed in 1726, and in 1735 the Grand Lodge of France was formed in Paris. In 1756 fourteen private Lodges formed a Grand Lodge in the Netherlands. Although Freemasonry was generally popular and grew rapidly, there were periods in France and the Netherlands when Masonic activity was prohibited by law. Exclusive meetings, a large body of secret material, and serious oaths taken on the scriptures were considered to be a potential threat to the authority of the Church and the government. Eventually, as members of the nobility became Masons and as the governments came to understand the nature of Freemasonry, these prohibitions were lifted; and the Order continued to grow. In Germany, which at that time was a group of Principalities, the philosophical teachings of Freemasonry were apparently attractive to many of the Princes, and Freemasonry prospered there. Generally speaking, there was a Grand Lodge in each Principality; they have consolidated to fewer since. We consider this development on the Continent of Europe in greater detail later in the book.

As we are reminded by those early Lodges in Gibraltar and India, the 18th century was also a period of active colonial expansion for many of the

The English apron opposite dates to just before the formation of UGLE in 1813. At this time the apron was not used to designate a Brother's Masonic rank. Instead, aprons displayed some beautiful artistic renderings of various Masonic symbols. The figures here represent Faith, Hope and Charity, with Charity the highest.

Freemasonry has always inspired great creativity on the part of
its members. This intriguing drawing – dated 'June 25 1802' –
was created by a Brother who has recorded the symbols of the
Craft in such a way that he can contemplate them and relive
the experience of receiving the Degrees. The meaning of the
monogram in the centre is unclear. It may be that the artist has
encrypted some words that capture the essence of his experience.
Cryptography is sometimes used by Masons (see pp. 266–71).

June 25. 1802.

THE GIFT OF PETER RING FACT 1777

As Freemasonry has grown throughout the world, it has left a fascinating material culture. Freemasons took great pleasure in decorating useful objects with symbols of the Order. Opposite is a wonderful board in marquetry, showing the Temple, as well as familiar motifs such as the rough and perfect ashlars. Another depiction of the Temple appears on the snuff box, right, which also has a dramatic 'G' in a Blazing Star. The powder horn below is beautifully and laboriously decorated with Masonic scenes, and it was probably made for use in an army or navy Lodge. The small, hand-decorated box below, meanwhile, contains a picture of the Brazen Serpent, and a sword – probably Templar images, though also associated with the Scottish Rite.

LE GENIE DU COMPAGNONNAGE FAISANT LE TOUR DU GLOBE.

Par le travail,
le zèle,
la bienfaisance,
la justice,

la prudence
et la conduite
on parvient
à ce mérite.

PAR CHARUE, PIERRE DIT BOURGUIGNON LE BIEN ZÉLÉ C. C. B. D. D.
PROPRIÉTÉ DÉPOSÉE.

European countries and the Masons that went to those colonies took their Freemasonry with them. This expansion covered a very large geographical area. Speaking generally, in the eastern hemisphere Freemasonry was introduced to all the English, French and Dutch colonies in Africa, India, Burma, Indonesia, Australia, New Zealand and South East Asia, and eventually into Japan. In the western hemisphere Freemasonry was introduced first to the English colonies in North America, and then to the European colonies in the Caribbean Islands and Central and South America.

The explosive growth of Masonry in Britain and on the Continent of Europe, followed by the formation of a second Grand Lodge in England, introduced a question we have touched on above and which has continued to this day. How was a Brother who was travelling to know that the Masonic Lodge that he was about to visit was, in fact, a Lodge that followed the proper principles of Freemasonry? And how was that Lodge to know that the visiting Brother was a proper Mason? This raises the question of 'regularity', which has many implications. Although Freemasonry is to be found throughout the world, it is not a single 'worldwide organization'. The official governing body of Freemasonry is the Grand Lodge; and as we have seen, there is usually a Grand Lodge in each country. These Grand Lodges recognize each other and acknowledge each other's authority because they all adhere to the same set of principles. Generally speaking, these principles have virtually been in effect since the founding of the Order. In 1929 they were summarized by UGLE as follows:

- A new Grand Lodge must have been established by a regular Grand Lodge.

- The belief in a Supreme Being is required for membership. The name of that Supreme Being and the manner in which It is to be worshiped is the business of the individual member.

- All Initiates take their Obligations on, or in full view of, the open Volume of Sacred Law which the Initiate considers to be sacred.

The issue of 'regularity' in Freemasonry is an important one, since it concerns the fundamental philosophy of the Order. In France there are several different Grand Lodges – above is the Lodge jewel for the French National Grand Lodge, which clearly displays its close ties to the United States and England, thus pronouncing itself to be 'regular'. Yet Freemasons remember that deep down they are all Brothers – the image opposite, titled 'The Spirit of Brotherhood Makes the Earth Turn', shows unity and brotherhood between all men.

Once they have been initiated, Freemasons are able to visit recognized Lodges anywhere in the world. For this reason, the Mason's certificate is very important, offering an introduction. The certificate opposite is from early 20th-century Spain – before 1928, when Freemasonry was outlawed in that country. Happily, that period of oppression in Spain has passed, and the Order has progressively revived. Few parts of the world have been completely untouched by Freemasonry at one time or other – the enamel jewel above comes from a Lodge in Kosovo, in the Balkans.

- The membership shall consist exclusively of men.

- The Grand Lodge shall have sovereign jurisdiction over its subordinate Lodges.

- The Three Great Lights of Freemasonry (the Volume of Sacred Law, the Square, and the Compasses) shall be displayed when a Grand Lodge, or a subordinate Lodge, is at work.

- The discussion of religion and politics within a Lodge is prohibited.

- The Antient Landmarks, customs and usages of the Craft are to be strictly observed.

- If a Grand Lodge adheres to these principles, it is considered to be 'regular'.

As Freemasonry spread throughout the world, the various countries in which Grand Lodges were established had very different cultural environments; and as a result the local Masonic organizations sometimes had very different priorities. Occasionally a departure from these principles was considered by local Masons to be appropriate, and an example will illustrate the point. In some European countries in the 18th century social reform was an important issue, and political issues were discussed in some Lodges. It must be acknowledged that many of the social reforms that have been accomplished by Freemasons have been of very great benefit. For example, the Grand Orient of France was largely responsible for the introduction of secular education in France, and that has been of significant benefit to a very large number of people. Nonetheless, the discussion of political issues in Lodges can cause animosity among the Brethren; and it can also bring Freemasonry under suspicion of anti-government activities with subsequent prohibition of meetings. Because of these concerns Grand Lodges that permit Masonic participation in political activities are not considered to be 'regular', and the members of 'regular' Grand Lodges are not permitted to have Masonic intercourse with them.

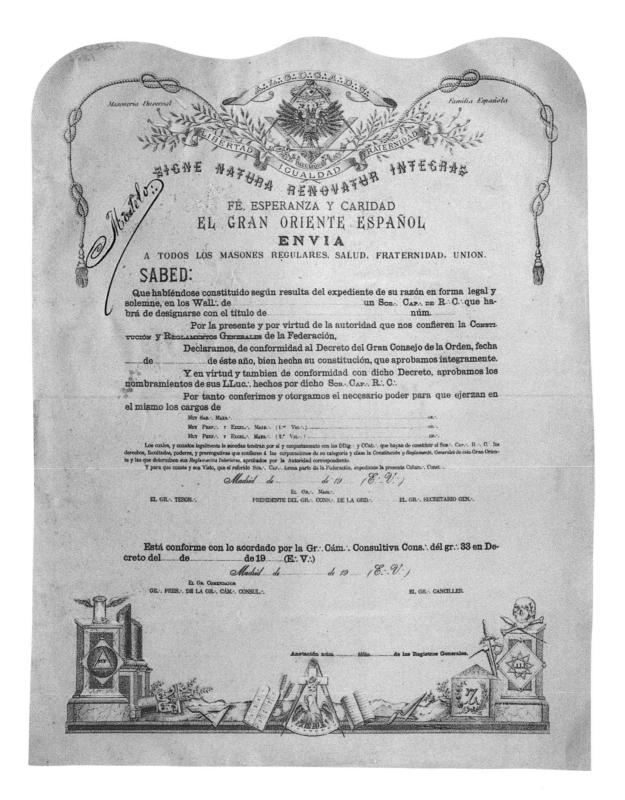

A∴ L∴ G∴ D∴ G∴ A∴ D∴ U∴

Masoneria Universal

Familia Española

LIBERTAD   IGUALDAD   FRATERNIDAD

Modelo

AIGNE NATURA RENOVATUR INTEGRAE

FÉ, ESPERANZA Y CARIDAD
EL GRAN ORIENTE ESPAÑOL
ENVIA
A TODOS LOS MASONES REGULARES, SALUD, FRATERNIDAD, UNION.

SABED:

Que habiéndose constituido según resulta del expediente de su razón en forma legal y solemne, en los Wall∴ de _____ un Sob∴ Cap∴ de R∴ C∴ que habrá de designarse con el título de _____ núm.

Por la presente y por virtud de la autoridad que nos confieren la Constitución y Reglamentos Generales de la Federación,

Declaramos, de conformidad al Decreto del Gran Consejo de la Orden, fecha _____ de _____ de éste año, bien hecha su constitución, que aprobamos integramente.

Y en virtud y tambien de conformidad con dicho Decreto, aprobamos los nombramientos de sus LLuc∴ hechos por dicho Sob∴ Cap∴ R∴ C∴:

Por tanto conferimos y otorgamos el necesario poder para que ejerzan en el mismo los cargos de

Muy Sab∴ Maes∴ _____ gr∴.
Muy Perf∴ y Excel∴ Maes∴ (1.ª Vig∴.) _____ gr∴.
Muy Perf∴ y Excel∴ Maes∴ (2.ª Vig∴.) _____ gr∴.

Los cuales, y cuantos legalmente le sucedan tendran por sí y conjuntamente con las DDig∴ y CCab∴ que hayan de constituir el Sob∴ Cap∴ R∴ C∴ los derechos, facultades, poderes, y prerrogativas que confieren á las corporaciones de su categoría y clase la Constitución y Reglamentos Generales de éste Gran Oriente y las que determinen sus Reglamentos Interiores, aprobados por la Autoridad correspondiente.

Y para que conste y sea Visto, que el referido Sob∴ Cap∴ forma parte de la Federación, expedimos la presente Colum∴ Const∴

Madrid de _____ de 19 ___ (E∴ V∴)

El Gr∴ Maes∴
EL GR∴ TESOR∴   PRESIDENTE DEL GR∴ CONS∴ DE LA ORD∴   EL GR∴ SECRETARIO GEN∴

Está conforme con lo acordado por la Gr∴ Cám∴ Consultiva Cons∴ dél gr∴ 33 en Decreto del _____ de _____ de 19 ___ (E∴ V∴)

Madrid de _____ de 19 ___ (E∴ V∴)

El Gr∴ Comendador
GR∴ PRES∴ DE LA GR∴ CÁM∴ CONSUL∴   EL GR∴ CANCILLER

Anotación núm _____ fólio _____ de los Registros Generales.

Throughout the 19th and early 20th centuries Freemasonry was very fashionable, and prominent members of society participated in its activities. In recent years this popularity has declined. Perhaps this is because of the fact that Masons have been giving their attention to charities and to social activities and have not been focusing on the philosophical teachings of the Order. If that be the case, the present period presents a good opportunity for Freemasonry. That is because among young people in Western societies there is an increasing interest in a metaphysics that is compatible with the Hermetic/Cabbalistic tradition. Grand Lodges that have chosen to emphasize that aspect of the Order have noticed the increase in interest. We will look at an overview of this teaching in due course; we will also consider how the teachings of Freemasonry have become available to women. There is a promising future here.

Ultimately, Freemasonry is about the commitment of the individual to improve himself, as suggested by the print opposite that describes the moral aspects of the Working Tools. And clearly many men have drawn great inspiration from their Masonic work: the Master's jewel above, for example, which shows a charming Art Nouveau influence, is a miniature work of art. The Beehives overleaf are symbols of industrious labour, appropriate to Freemasonry since work in the hive, as in Freemasonry, is interior work.

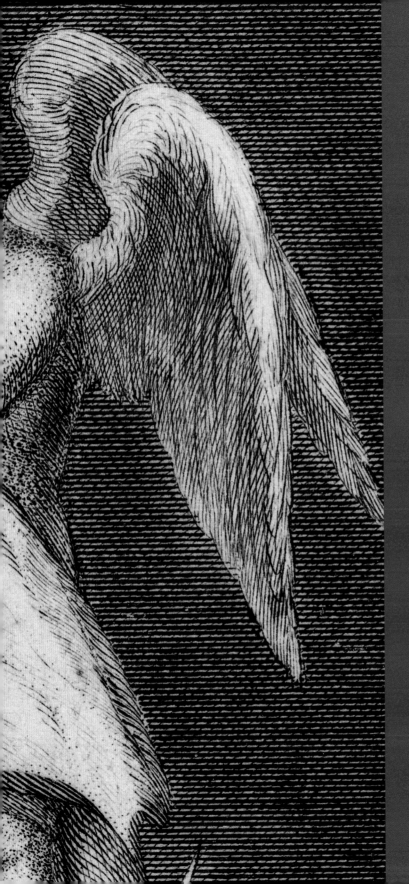

1

The Broken Column

THE DAWN OF FREEMASONRY

The Broken Column symbolizes the fall of Man – the figure of Time pulls the hair of the girl who mourns Hiram Abiff, the architect of the Temple of Solomon. His story lies at the root of Freemasonry.

THE ORIGIN of Freemasonry is one of history's greatest puzzles. The operative craft of stonemasons, the Knights Templar, the architects and craftsmen who built King Solomon's Temple, and even the Mystery cults of the ancient world have all been proposed as sources of the Order. More recent studies, however, have shown that much of the philosophical grounding of Freemasonry stems from the Renaissance, an intriguing blend of mystical traditions such as Cabbala and Hermeticism given a symbolic structure derived from the medieval craft guilds.

Since the very beginning of formal Freemasonry there has been vigorous discussion as to the philosophical source of the ritual dramas and symbolism used in the Degrees. *The Defence of Masonry*, an anonymous work first published in 1730 and included in the 1738 printing of Anderson's *Constitutions*, advances the idea that Freemasonry is a direct descendant of the Mystery cults of classical Greece and Rome – that stonemasons over the ages had somehow preserved and passed on the arcane knowledge and esoteric secrets of the ancient world. This idea was restated by the American Masonic scholar Albert Pike in his classic and influential 19th-century work, *Morals and Dogma*.

However, from the opposite perspective, writers such as Henry Wilson Coil, a 33° Mason and author of the much respected *Masonic Encyclopedia*, first published in 1961, take the view that the idea of a Masonic connection with the Ancient Mysteries is impossible and that such an interpretation of the symbolism of Freemasonry is foolishness.

In the 18th century, when formal Freemasonry began, many, such as this artist in Frankfurt in 1738, saw Freemasons as responsible for the monuments of the ancient world, partly because Masonic imagery often uses Classical architecture. Note the aprons, working tools on the ground, and the broken column to the left.

At the time, Coil and the other opponents of the idea of classical influence had some good arguments on their side. There is no evidence of any unbroken connection between the builders of the classical world and those of the mid-1600s, and in any case any organization suspected of harbouring important secrets would not have made it past the Church's Inquisition.

On the other hand, even while Coil's *Encyclopedia* was being published, Frances A. Yates was examining the history of thought during the Renaissance, that revival of classical learning that took root in Italy in the 14th century. Through her studies, she determined that the essence of Renaissance philosophy was a body of thought which she called the 'Hermetic/Cabbalistic tradition'. Her historical research was to change our understanding of Renaissance Europe, demonstrating that, as well as the important developments made in art and architecture (which included the rediscovery of Vitruvius), the Renaissance also introduced a profound change in European intellectual activity. It is my hypothesis that Freemasonry is a codification of that Hermetic/Cabbalistic tradition, and it might be useful to take the time to examine this idea.

The intellectual capital of Italy during the Renaissance was Florence, and by the late 1400s we find evidence of both of

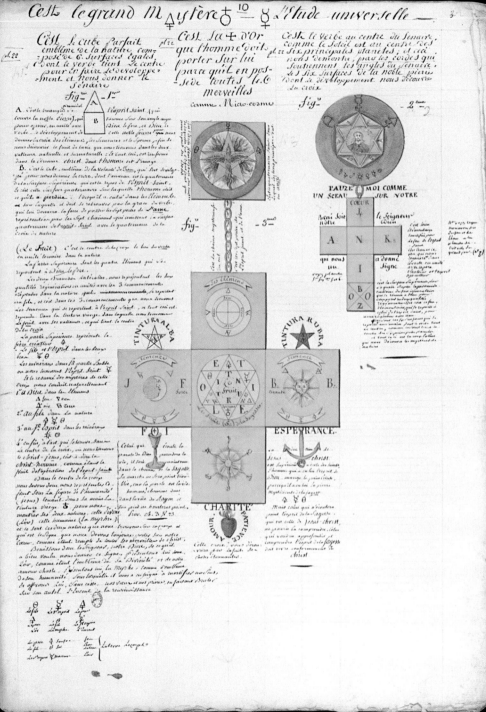

these traditions there. The first was influenced by the *Hermetica*, a work of Egyptian philosophy with a heavy Hellenistic and Christian influence. It was written in Alexandria in the 2nd century AD, though it was attributed to Hermes Trismegistus, the principal character of the work and thought to be a contemporary of Moses. The second was Cabbala, the mystical tradition of Judaism. Combined, they gave rise to a philosophy in which, in addition to seeking the salvation of one's soul after death, one can also ascend in consciousness from the physical world through the levels of the psyche/soul and the spirit and experience the Divine Presence while one is incarnate. That, of course, was the intent of the practitioner of the Ancient Mysteries. This theme was followed by many of the serious thinkers of the Renaissance. The writings of Francesco Giorgi, a Franciscan monk in Venice, Johannes Reuchlin and Cornelius Agrippa, both German philosophers, and John Dee and Elias Ashmole, both British scholars, provide examples that cover the period from about 1500 to 1650 and a geographical area from Northern Italy, through Central Europe to Britain. Therefore it seems reasonable to conclude that the source of the Freemasons' interest in classical philosophy was their study of the Renaissance philosophers. And Ashmole, as we saw in the Introduction, was one of the very first Freemasons.

The new interest in the Hermetic tradition also fed a movement with even more obscure origins than Free-

masonry – the so-called 'Rosicrucian Enlightenment'. This secret, deeply mystical Order, which appeared to be based largely in Germany, first came to widespread attention through three publications in the early 1600s, but aside from these works there is little to prove that it existed as a true group of initiates. However, Yates in particular has argued that the currents that led to the philosophy of the Rosicrucians – and here we are talking of the same interest in Hermeticism and mystical traditions – almost certainly led to Freemasonry.

Yet Freemasonry differed in one crucial way – in its obvious debt to the organizational structure of stonemasons' guilds. The precise nature of the relationship between operative and speculative masons is unclear, though well into the 19th century many Freemasons looked to the 'Old Charges' – a group of medieval manuscripts that deal with the organization of operative Lodges – for guidance in ritual and jurisprudence, use of passwords, and so forth.

Another theory that has enjoyed a new popularity recently has been the idea that the Freemasons are the direct descendants of the Knights Templar – again probably inspired by the Masons' secrecy. While this hypothesis has been discredited by respected authorities, the Rosslyn Chapel in Scotland – long associated with the Templars – is held in high esteem by Freemasons. But for most it is the *philosophical* link with the Templars that is important.

The Classical god Mercury can be found depicted throughout European history, often with magical overtones – here he appears on a Masonic jewel worn by a Junior Deacon. The image opposite is a French attempt to codify the universe, dating probably to the 18th century. Building on Rosicrucian mystical thought and sacred geometries, it also features symbols found in Freemasonry.

THE LEGENDARY ORIGINS OF FREEMASONRY

This 19th-century French print, entitled *The Origin of Freemasonry*, is a romantic interpretation showing the origins of the Order to be in ancient times. The caption explains that the scene shows the period after the Great Flood, when 'seventeen wise men built the ancient monuments' (including those of Egypt, Rome and Greece), presumably to new and divinely inspired plans. Thus, the Freemasons are seen as responsible for God's new, perfect, world. To the right are personifications of Faith, Hope and Charity, while various Masonic images appear throughout – the ladder with seven rungs, the terrestrial and celestial globes, and the tools in the left foreground. Meanwhile, the eye of the Great Architect of the Universe oversees all...

SHALL BUILD ME AN HOUSE AND

SOLOMON

HIRAM

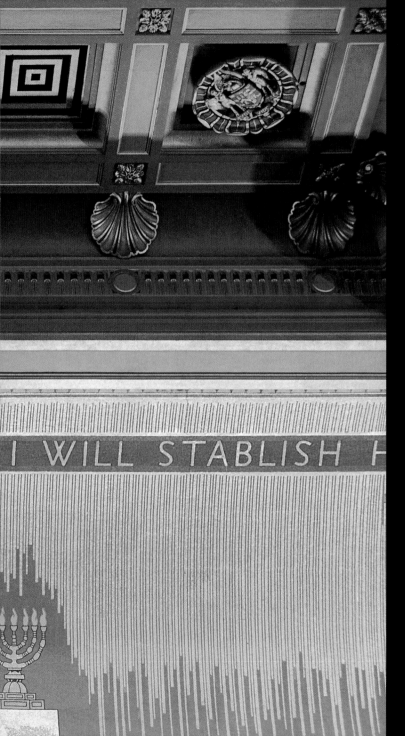

In seeking a historical background for their Order, many early Freemasons traced their roots to the building of King Solomon's Temple. Aside from Solomon himself, the key figure in the story is the architect, Hiram Abiff, who features prominently in the ritual of two of the three Degrees. Here, in the mosaic architrave of the Grand Temple in Freemasons' Hall, London, he is depicted with Solomon, again with the ladder with seven rungs (see the preceding spread) and emblems of Faith, Hope and Charity. At the bottom of the ladder is the Ark of the Covenant, an important symbol in some of the Higher Degrees.

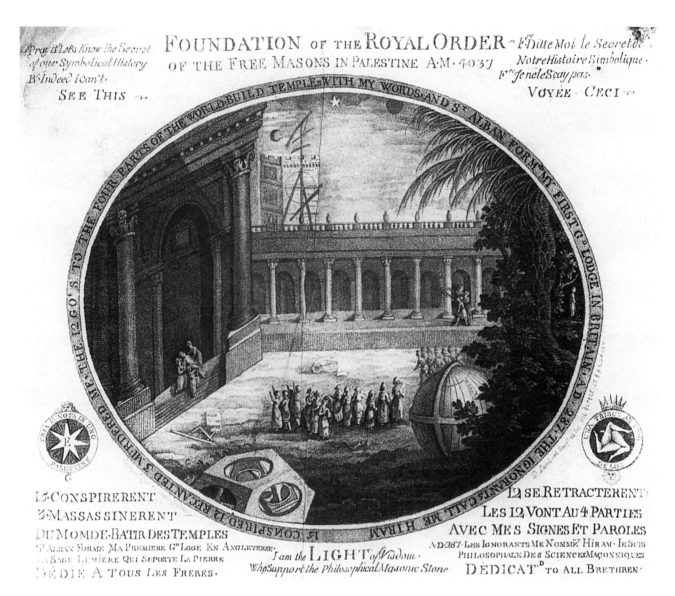

FOUNDATION OF THE ROYAL ORDER OF THE FREE MASONS IN PALESTINE A·M·4037

Pray B⸴ Lets Know the Secret of our Symbolical History
B⸴ Indeed I can't·
SEE THIS

F⸴ Ditte Moi le Secret⸴
NotreHistoire Simbolique·
F⸴ Je ne le Scay pas·
VOYÉE CECI

THE 12 G O⸴ S TO THE FOUR PARTS OF THE WORLD·BUILD TEMPLE·WITH MY WORDS·AND S⸴ ALBAN FORM MY FIRST G⸴ LODGE IN BRITAIN A·D· 1186 LONDON·18 JULI·1786 13 CONSPIRED & RETAINED S MURDERED ME·CALL ME HIRAM

I⸴ CONSPIRERENT
& MASSASSINERENT
DU MOMDE·BATIR DES TEMPLES
S⸴ ALBAN FORME MA PREMIERE G⸴ LOGE EN ANGLETERRE·
LA SAGE LUMIÉRE QUI SUPORTE LA PIERRE
DÉDIE A TOUS LES FRERES·

I am the LIGHT of Wisdom·
Who Support the Philosophical Masonic Stone·

12 SE RETRACTERENT
LES 12 VONT AU 4 PARTIES
AVEC MES SIGNES ET PAROLES
A·D·287· LES IGNORANTS ME NONMÉ⸴ HIRAM· JE SUIS
PHILOSOPHALE DES SCIENCES MAÇONNIQUES
DÉDICAT⸴ TO ALL BRETHREN·

The legend of the murder of Hiram Abiff communicates one of the central teachings of Freemasonry. Those of a literal turn of mind have used it as a theory of the origin of the Order, as indicated in the print above, but that is unlikely: Hiram's murder is a Masonic symbol, but there is no evidence that it is an historical fact. The Biblical account of the Temple indicates that Hiram completed all of his work for Solomon (I Kings, 7:40). According to Masonic legend, Hiram's murderers, shown in the drawing to the right, were slain at the command of King Solomon. The acacia branch, meanwhile, is a symbol of rebirth.

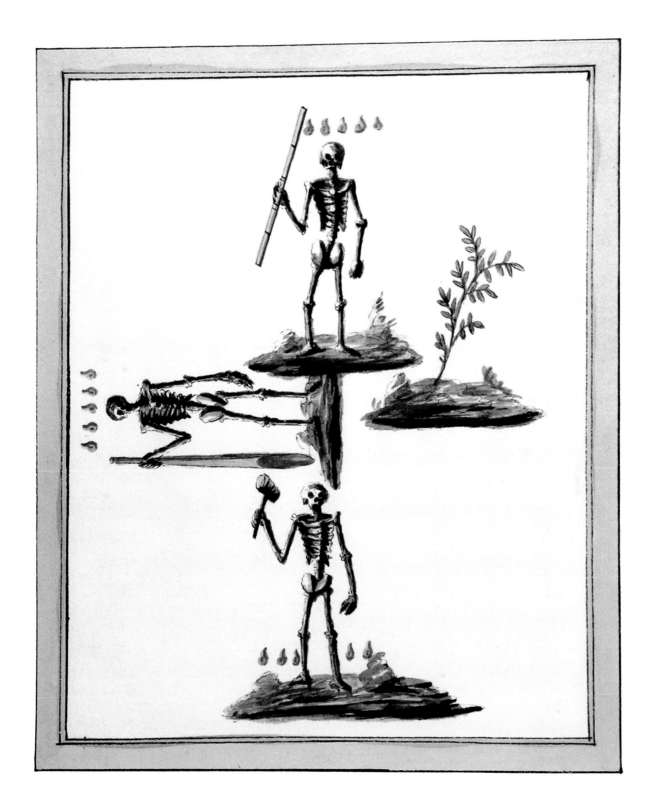

The Egyptian Rite.

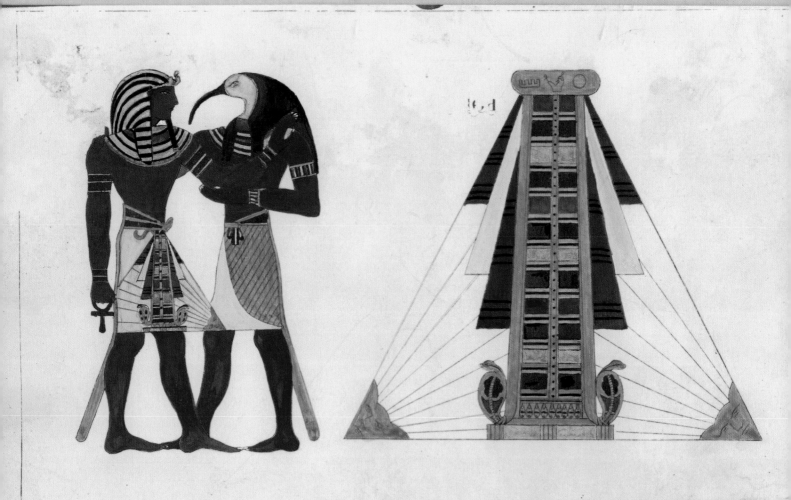

Pharaoh Ouserei in masonic communication with the High Grand Master disguised in Ibis mask. He has just been invested with the triangular masonic apron, surmounted by the Apron of Serpents, emblem of Royalty & Symbol of The Fall. He also grasps the Grand Masonic Emblem, or Key of Life.

The Ancient Mysteries from Egypt and Greece have often been thought to be the source of Freemasonry. The 'Egyptian Rite' shown opposite certainly attempts to make a case for Freemasonry in ancient times (note the ladder design on the 'apron'), but the author has clearly gone a little too far – as has the artist above in his imagined depiction of an initiation (the mason's tools engraved in the walls are an unlikely touch). The Greek relief right depicts a critical moment in a genuine ceremony of initiation from the ancient world. Demeter gives corn to Triptolemos, an initiate who will bestow benefit (of which this gift is symbolic) on mankind. The classical initiations involved rituals which are perhaps not dissimilar to those of Freemasonry, but it is more reasonable to understand that Masonic ideas were derived from the revival of antiquity in the Renaissance than from antiquity directly.

There are a number of mystical structures in the Bible, all of which have been attributed to the Freemasons at some point. Solomon's Temple we have already encountered; others include Noah's Ark and the Tower of Babel (seen being constructed right in a French medieval manuscript). The manuscript opposite dates to the 18th century and is probably Viennese. The reference to Mercury in the text below the scene of the building of the Tower of Babel conflates Biblical and classical stories. At the architect's feet are Masonic working tools. The little sign to the left of the caption is derived from John Dee's *Monas Hieroglyphica* (see p. 73), a sure sign of Hermetic influence.

JACQUES DE MOLAI

Dernier Grand Maître

des Templiers

Brulé à Paris, le 19 Mars 1313.

Locerf sculp.

The Knights Templar were a Christian Order established in 1118 to protect pilgrims travelling to and from the Holy Land. Over time they built many churches, often circular (as with the Temple Church in London, opposite), in imitation of the Church of the Holy Sepulchre in Jerusalem. They also acquired great wealth and influence and eventually jealousy led to their downfall. Jacques de Molay, pictured left, was the last Grand Master of the Templar Order. He was accused of heresy, and his execution by burning in 1314 was the culmination of the persecution of Templars in France.

The Templars were first proposed as the forerunners of Freemasonry in the early 18th century. The idea was that many of the Knights left France to avoid prosecution in the 14th century, and went to Scotland where, in time, they became Freemasons. There is not much evidence to support this hypothesis, but the Templars probably made a contribution to the Masonic Order indirectly. With their strong connection to the Middle East they, and the mystical orientation they are said to have had, would have had a significant influence on European thought, perhaps paving the way for the interest in mystical traditions seen in the Renaissance.

The Rosslyn Chapel, opposite, is one of
the most curious structures in Scotland.
The foundation was laid in 1446, and its
stonework is among the most elaborate
and beautiful in the world. There are many
legends associated with the Chapel. Among
them is the idea that the Holy Grail and
other Christian treasures, originally in
possession of the Knights Templar, are
hidden in a vault in the crypt which has
been sealed for centuries. More probably
the crypt contains the remains of the
St Clairs, the family who undertook the
chapel's construction. Sir William St Clair
(above), a later member of the St Clair
family, was made Hereditary Grand Master
Mason of Scotland in 1736. The 18th
century also saw the emergence of the
Masonic Knights Templar Order (see pp.
192–5), which, though unconnected to
the medieval Order revived much of its
forerunner's iconography, as seen in this
19th-century jewel.

onmc labia mca a

In the Middle Ages the stonemason's Lodge was a shed on the building site where the craftsmen could work, rest, organize their activities and sometimes sleep. The stonemason's guilds had passwords that permitted craftsmen to travel and identify themselves as masons so that they could work on remote building sites. Today's speculative Freemasonry derives most of its symbols from the operative Craft. For example,

the board above shows Euclid's 47th Proposition (top left), which would have been very useful to the operative craftsman in enabling him to construct a right angle. All of the tools shown on the board are derived from the stonemason's craft.

Geometry was often viewed as an attribute of the Divine
in the Middle Ages, as can be seen in the manuscript image
opposite of God drawing the Universe with compasses.
Such beliefs accord with the Masonic conception of the
'Great Architect of the Universe', the creative principle
that governs everything. Above is a more down-to-earth
reminder of the Freemasons' supposed heritage, a clock
decorated with Masonic symbols and with a stonemason
cutting the ashlar as the seconds pass…

Cy comence la bible en francois translatee celon les hystoires escolastres. Et premierement
le liure de genesis. du quel le premier chapi
tre parle de la creacion du monde. Et pmie
ment de la creacion du ael. et de la terre.
Au comencement crea dieu
le ael et la terre. Si estoit

mencement par le quel et ou quel le pere
crea le monde. Et Le monde est dit en .iij.
manieres. Aucune fois est le monde appelez
le ael empyree. glose. Les theologiens dient
que en la region du ael. cest en paradis sont

Freemasonry makes great use of symbolism derived from classical architecture, in particular the 'Orders'. These were first classified by the Roman architect Vitruvius, whose writings were greatly admired and emulated during the Renaissance. The image to the right was drawn by Renaissance architect Vincenzo Scamozzi, and shows five orders – from left to right, Tuscan, Doric, Ionic, Corinthian and Composite (here called 'Romano'). The Renaissance saw a dramatic increase in the status of the architect, since, as Vitruvius had indicated, the architect should be able to draw and be knowledgeable in the subjects of philosophy, history, arithmetic, geometry, music, medicine, jurisprudence and astronomy. All of these skills are embraced by the Liberal Arts and Sciences, which were the basis of education at the time.

The certificate opposite with its image of St Paul's Cathedral depicts three of the orders mentioned above, Doric, Ionic and Corinthian (the ones used in Greek as opposed to Roman architecture). On top of the columns are personifications of the three Cardinal Virtues – Faith, Hope and Charity.

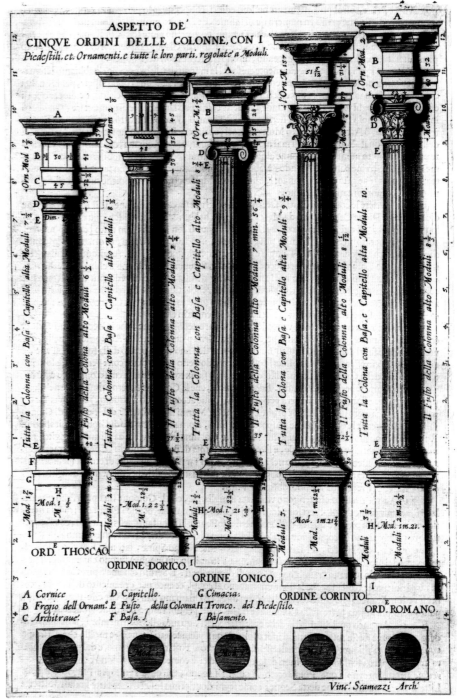

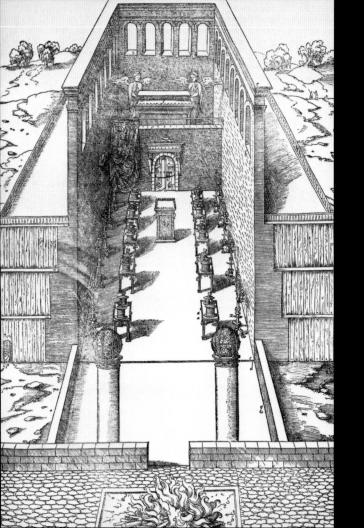

The Renaissance saw the growth of interest in mystical architecture, and in accurate reconstructions of Biblical structures. The image on the left is a reconstruction of the inner part of Solomon's Temple, though like all such pictures, it remains a speculation on the nature of that edifice. Not surprisingly, for a work of the 16th century, there is a marked similarity to the design of the European cathedrals and major churches of the period (with four clearly divided hierarchical spaces representing the Physical World, the World of the Soul, the World of the Spirit, and the Divine World). All Lodges, of course, emulate Solomon's Temple, but in this case the similarity is pronounced, with the two

EORVNDEM
CASTRORVM
DISPOSITIO, MVNDVM
referens, & Templum.

Genes. 48. ℣. 5. & Cap. 49. ℣. 4. 7. 9. 13. 14. 17. 19. 21. Deut. 33. ℣. 26.

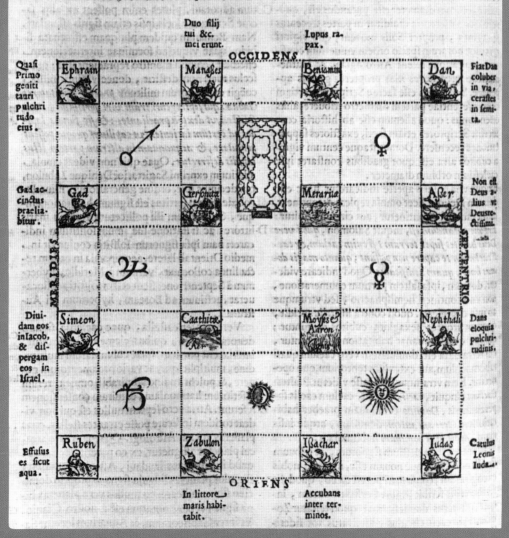

Fasciculus Chemicus :
OR
Chymical Collections.
EXPRESSING
The Ingreſs, Progreſs, and Egreſs,
of the Secret Hermetick Science,
out of the choiſeſt and moſt
Famous Authors.

Collected and digeſted in ſuch an
order, that it may prove to the advantage,
not onely of the Beginners, but Proficients
of this high Art, by none hither-
to diſpoſed in this Method.

Whereunto is added, The Arcanum or
Grand Secret of Hermetick Philoſophy.

Both made Engliſh
By James Haſolle, Eſquire,
Qui eſt Mercuriophilus Anglicus.

Our Magiſtry is begun and perfetted, by onely one
things namely, Mercury. Ventur. p.26.

London, Printed by J. Fleſher for Richard Mynne,
at the ſign of St. Paul in Little Britain. 1650.

The Renaissance saw a great rise in interest in mystical and alchemical philosophies. The Cabbalistic 'Tree of Life' opposite dates to the 16th century, and is a representation of Adam Kadmon, the Primordial Being of Divinity which began when the Deity willed Itself into existence. The influence of Cabbala is also reflected in the illustration on the title page of *Chymical Collections* (above), a group of works on alchemy published in 1650. In that drawing, as in the Tree of Life, there are three columns. The column on the right contains objects relating to action – in this case illustrated by military activity; the column on the left contains objects relating to restraint and understanding – represented by intellectual activity; and the objects on the central column relate to the conscious awareness of Divine Principles by which the two can be held in balance. The ideal of opposites with a balancing agency is represented in an archetypal sense at the top of the drawing. The Sun and the Moon remained prominent symbols in Freemasonry.

The Rosicrucian Order is one of the most curious puzzles in the history of Europe. Claiming to have been begun in the 15th century by Christian Rosenkreutz, who had travelled in the East and brought back vital esoteric knowledge, almost certainly it actually began in the 17th century, but may never have existed as a functioning Order at all – only as a philosophical idea. There are three 'authentic' Rosicrucian documents published in three successive years, two manifestos – the *Fama Fraternitatis*, and the *Confessio Fraternitatis* from 1614 and 1615 – and finally *The Chemical Wedding of Christian Rosenkreutz*, in 1616. The Order appears to have been dedicated to the study of nature in order to gain spiritual insight. It seems also to have been concerned with

arithmetic, geometry, alchemy, and the advancement of knowledge and interior work toward spiritual enlightenment. Their interest in alchemy was philosophical, and some have remarked on similarities with Freemasonry's 'alchemy of the spirit'. The Rosicrucian Ritual (left) may be a speculation on the Order's workings or it could be a ritual from one of the many imitative Orders which were founded in sympathy with the movement. The French certificate above is Masonic, but, just as with the Knights Templar, shows Freemasons referencing other Orders – in this case through the inclusion of the rose and cross motif. The Rose Croix degree is the 18th Degree in the Scottish Rite, and there is an Order of Masonic Rosicrucians (see p. 211).

1604

Both of these images come from a German Masonic publication on Rosicrucian imagery from the late 18th century, showing an early interest in the Order among Freemasons. The 'Secret Rosicrucian Figure' to the left contains symbols which provide information about the Order. The date, 1604, if it can be trusted, is before the publication of the *Fama*, which indicates that it is an early image. The figure has the four levels characteristic of the mystical ascent. The second level, the psyche or Soul, contains various alchemical symbols, and the Crown in the Heavens indicates the aspiration toward experience of the Divine Presence. Opposite, meanwhile, is a figure containing astrological, as well as alchemical, references. The diagram under the cup in the centre is derived from John Dee's *Monas Hieroglyphica*, an important mystical work, and the choice of planets, Venus and Jupiter, planets relating to activity on the right, and Mars and Saturn, planets relating to restraint on the left, has a definite Cabbalistic connotation.

TABULA SMARAGDINA HERMETIS.

VISITA INTERIORA TERRÆ RECTIFICANDO INVENIES OCCULTUM LAPIDEM

VERBA SECRETORUM HERMETIS.

2

Rebuilding the Temple

THE HISTORY OF FREEMASONRY

In 1723, six years after the founding of the first Grand Lodge, James Anderson published the Constitutions of Freemasonry, the first written regulations relating to the Order (the frontispiece of which is shown here). They set out – and made public – the principles upon which the Order was founded.

THE PROPER HISTORY of Freemasonry begins in an ale house in London in 1717. Within thirty years the Order had spread to almost every country in Western Europe, and soon after to overseas colonies, including India, China and, perhaps most importantly, North America. Though it faced persecution from governments and the Church, by the 19th century it had become truly global.

However uncertain Freemasonry's history was before 1717, the establishment of the premier Grand Lodge in that year formally created the Order and changed its fortunes radically. Of particular importance was the third Grand Master, installed in 1719, John Theophilus Desagulier. He was a Huguenot clergyman who had escaped religious persecution in France and had a serious interest in scientific experimentation. He was a Fellow of the Royal Society, and attracted members of the intellectual community to Freemasonry. Four years later the Duke of Montagu became Grand Master, and the presence of nobility at the head of the Order caused a substantial increase in public interest. Masonic events began to be reported in the press. New Lodges were being formed; and as more of these new Lodges were located in the provinces, the Grand Lodge began to constitute Provincial Grand Lodges, in England and in overseas territories, to administer local Lodges.

The increased public interest also caused problems for the Grand Lodge. In the 1720s exposures began to appear, claiming to reveal the practices and secrets of Freemasonry. Perhaps the most serious of these was written in 1730 by Samuel Prichard, whose exposure detailed the entire ritual he had experienced. In reaction to this exposure, and to prevent access to Lodges by persons who were not Masons, in 1739 the Grand Lodge exchanged the words of recogni-

Here the arms of the 'Antient' Grand Lodge, formed in 1751, show an interest in metaphysics. The Man, the Eagle, the Lion and the Ox, the archetypal inhabitants of the Four Worlds, are quartered in the shield.

tion associated with the first two Degrees. This change was to have an unanticipated effect. In the 1740s there were many Irish Masons in England who had been initiated in Irish Lodges. Since they were unable to enter local Lodges because of the changed words, they formed Lodges of their own and in 1751 formed their own Grand Lodge. This new organization called itself the Antient Grand Lodge because it claimed its working to be the original, ancient, Masonic practice. The 'Antients' referred to the premier Grand Lodge (actually many years older than the Antients) as 'the Moderns' because of the changes they were said to have made to traditional practices. This confusing nomenclature was to last for many years. In 1756 the Antients published their own constitution, *Ahiman Rezon*. The Antients originally represented Lodges in London, but through the efforts of Laurence Dermott, their very able and energetic Grand Secretary, they expanded very quickly in terms both of numbers and of geographical area. There was an intense, and sometimes bitter, rivalry between the Antients and the Moderns which lasted until the final reconciliation in 1813.

Following the organization of the premier Grand Lodge in 1717 Private Lodges, and subsequently Grand Lodges, were also formed in Ireland, Scotland and throughout northern Europe. As mentioned previously, the first French lodge, the Loge Au Louis d'Argent, was formed in 1726. This Lodge was recognized by the Grand Lodge of England in 1732, and in 1735 the Grand Lodge of France was formed in Paris. Freemasonry grew in France until 1766 when all Masonic activities were prohibited by law, because the secretive meetings were considered to be a threat to the government. Prohibitions of this nature were to occur throughout Northern Europe, but they were intermittent. Masonic activities were resumed in France in 1771, at which time the Grand Master was Louis-Philippe d'Orleans, a cousin of King Louis XVI. At the end of the 18th century the cream of the French intellectual community – men such as LaFayette, Voltaire, Mirabeau, Lavoisier and Montesquieu – had become Freemasons. Among French Freemasons there have been various interpretations on the Craft's teachings – particularly on the issue of admission of women and atheists – and these differing views caused some Lodges to withdraw from the original Grand Lodge and form new Grand Lodges. At the present time there are several Grand Lodges in France.

In the Netherlands the first Lodge was started in November, 1734 at a tavern in The Hague, and a second was founded in the same city in October, 1735. Almost immediately thereafter the government declared it unlawful for Masons to meet or for citizens to provide accommodation for such meetings. Once again, the characteristics of the Masonic organization had caused official concern in the government and the Church. By the mid-1740s this difficulty had been overcome, and the Grand Lodge of the Netherlands was formed in 1756. The number of its subordinate Lodges in the Netherlands grew quickly thereafter. Secular powers proved more receptive to Freemasonry than the Catholic Church, which issued a Papal Bull in 1738 forbidding members of the Church from becoming Freemasons.

In the German Principalities the situation for Freemasonry was somewhat different to that in France and the Netherlands. Many of the Princes, it seems, were themselves open to Masonic teachings, and it is said that some started Lodges by Royal Decree. Perhaps this is not surprising considering that Germany was the cradle of the Rosicrucian Enlightenment. Frederick II was initiated in Loge d'Homburg in 1738; when he became King of Prussia in 1740 he took Freemasonry 'under his protection', and the Order grew rapidly. Perhaps because Freemasonry in Germany started when there were many Principalities, each with its independent authority, there have been as many as fifteen Grand Lodges in Germany. Today there are at least five and while each retains its identity, most have joined together as the United Grand Lodges of Germany.

During the 18th and 19th centuries Freemasonry spread to the European colonies situated throughout the world. In the North American colonies there were Lodges chartered by both the Modern and the Antient Grand Lodges. There appears to have been some political orientation among the membership, and in 1776, when the American colonies declared independence, many of the Moderns, remaining loyal to the King, went to Canada. In the United States today all the Grand Lodges are of Antient origin; many use the title 'Ahiman Rezon' in their Constitutions. In any case, North America proved of one the most fertile grounds for Freemasonry, and by the early 20th century Masons there could be counted in their millions. As in other countries American Freemasonry had a strong material culture, and we find all manner of everyday items decorated with symbols of instruction and morality. America was also the home of Prince Hall Freemasonry, open initially exclusively to African Americans, and in 1801 was the birthplace of the Scottish Rite as it is known today. The numbers of Freemasons continued to rise up to the middle of the 20th century, but that century also saw some of the most savage repression of the Order, especially in Germany under Hitler and Spain under Franco.

From humble origins in 18th-century England, when the jewel above was made, Freemasonry has spread around the world to become a truly global fraternity. The apron opposite was worn by the Grand Master of Peru, and is very traditional. The initials of the Grand Lodge of Peru are integrated on the flap.

B. Cole Sculp.

The premier Grand Lodge was founded in 1717 at a meeting of four Lodges at The Goose and Gridiron Ale House in St Paul's Churchyard, London. Sadly the actual building was pulled down at the end of the 19th century though the sign survived (see below). The name is said to have been a parody of the Swan and Lyre, a musical group that met there. The first Grand Master was Anthony Sayer, Gentleman (see right), elected at the meeting at which the Grand Lodge was founded. He died in 1741 and was honoured with a Masonic burial at St Paul's, Covent Garden.

Aside from Anderson's *Constitutions*, there were other 'unofficial' documents such as *A Book of the Ancient Constitutions of Free and Accepted Masons*, published in 1728 by Benjamin Cole and reprinted in 1731. Each of the Masons in the frontispiece holds a Masonic tool, a Square, the Compasses and a Plumbline; but this is a curious arrangement. Although the tools are all properly Masonic, the manner in which they are presented does not match usual Masonic practice. This uncertainty is characteristic of an 'unofficial work' and it has been observed many times since.

	St. Pauls Church-yard	every other Mond from y. 29.th of April inclusive
	Knaves Acre	every other Wedn from y 24.of April inclusive
	Turn ſtile	Firſt Wednesday in every Month
	Arundel ſtreet	Firſt Thursday in every Month
	Weſtminſter	Third Fryday in every Month
	Ivy lane	every other Thurs. from y 20 of June inclusive
	Newgate ſtreet	Firſt Monday in every Month
	Poultry	Second Wednesd in every Month
	Silver ſtreet	every other Fryd from y 26.of April inclusive
	in the Strand	Firſt Fryday in every Month

The 'Engraved List of Lodges' shown left was issued in 1723. It shows the signs of the various inns (including the Goose and Gridiron, top), where each Lodge met, as well as the days upon which they met. When a Lodge was constituted it had to forward its certificate to the Grand Secretary so that it could be included on the next Engraved List of Lodges. Lodges which did not do this were considered to be 'irregular', and its members would not be permitted to visit regular Lodges. This was the start of the long-running subject of 'regularity'. The Engraved List of Lodges shown opposite is of a later date and reflects the rapid rate at which Freemasonry grew after the founding of the Grand Lodge. This List shows the locations of 129 Lodges, some of which – numbers 51 (Gibraltar), 72 ('Bengall in the East Indies') and 90, (Louis d'Argent, Paris, not visible here) – were located overseas. By 1750 there were about two hundred Lodges in England alone.

27	28	29	30	Sr. Richard Steele	31	32	33	34	35	36	37	38	39
Stoke Newington	Salford near Manchester	Holborn	St. Bernard Street in Marid	Gibralter	Warwick	Leadenhall Street	Greek Street Soho	Henrietta Street near Covent Gard	Shorts Gardens	Red Lyon Street Holbourn	Corn Market Oxford	Scarburgh	Billingsgate	Cateton Street

47	48	49	50	5J	52	53	54	55	56	57	58	59	60	6J
Bloomsbury Market	Lijnn Regis in Norfolk	Cheap Side	Bengall in the East Indies	Lincoln	At the Beare and Harron in the Butcher Row	York Buildings	Old Baily	Jocky Fields	Bury St. Edmonds	Little St. Martin's Lane	Maccles field Cheshire	Bury St. Edmonds	Newgate Street	Smithfield

69	70	7J	72	73	74	75	76	77	78	79	80	8J	82	83
Fleetstreet	Antwerp Threedneedle Street	Rosemary Lane	Ludgate Street	Dorcett street Spittle Fields	White Ipswich	NEW INN Exeter	D. of Lorrain Suffolk Street	Fleetstreet	Butcher Row	upper Moore Fields	ROYAL VINE YARD St. James's Park	nyithout Temple Bar	Kryins Inn Darby	a Private Room Bolton Le Moors Lancashire

9J	92	93	94	95	96	97	98	99	100	J0J	J02	J03	J04	J05
City of Bath	in the Strand	Scotts Masons Lodge Devil Temple Bar	Masters Masons Lodge Butcher Ron	Masters Masons Lodge, Strand	Red Bury in Lancashier	Stourbridge Worcestersh	OATES'S COFFEE HOUSE Masters Lodg Great Whitt Street	SOLOMONS COFFEE HOUSE Pimblico	FORREST COFFEE HOUSE Charing Cross	P. O St. Saviours Deck Southwark	Hamburgh in Lower Saxony	Birmingham	Boston in New England	Valencien res in French Flanders

| JJ3 | JJ4 | JJ5 | JJ6 | JJ7 | JJ | JJ9 | J20 | J2J | J22 | J23 | J24 | J25 | J26 | J27 | J28 |

As Freemasonry spread, it always took on a local flavour – nowhere is this so evident as in aprons. An apron is the distinguishing badge of a Mason, and today a Mason's apron will indicate his Masonic rank; however, the original intent of the 'lambskin or white leather' apron was almost certainly to be a 'badge of innocence'. In any case, very quickly the plain white apron seemed to lose fashion and many early aprons, typically handmade, were beautifully decorated with the symbols of the Craft or Higher Degrees. The aprons shown here are from four different countries. Opposite is an Irish apron, with a comprehensive selection of symbols, many of which relate to Higher Degrees. The French apron, left, meanwhile, is far clearer and makes reference to the purpose of Freemasonry. The others are from Scotland (above left), and from the Netherlands (an elegant, classical composition). All date to the second half of the 18th century, or possibly the early 19th century.

Germany and Austria both proved very receptive to Freemasonry. The German jewel left is from Lodge Carl zu den 3 Aldren in Erfurt. The Lodge worked from 1814 to 1880. The Meissen 'Masonic Lovers' below, are both in Masonic regalia (she is sewing his apron). The presence of a pug dog suggests that this object may relate to the society of Mopses. This society was formed in Vienna after the Papal Bull of 1738 forbidding Catholics to be Freemasons (see p. 102). Catholic Masons, wishing to continue a fraternal relationship founded the androgynous Order of Mopses on 22 September, 1738. Although it retained some Masonic symbolism, it did not have Masonic affiliation. The 18th-century Certificate of Membership opposite, meanwhile, certifies that the holder is a member of a Lodge in Vienna.

WIR MEISTER VOM STVHL. DEPVTIRTER MEISTER.
Auffeher, Beamte und Mitglieder der von der Provinzial ☐
in Oesterreich rechtmäfsig conftituirten und vollkommenen ☐
☐ zur WAHRHEIT: entbieten allen unfern verei.
nigten, auch auf dem Erdboden zerftreuten Brüdern unfern
herzlichen Grufs. Erkennen den Ehrwürdigen Bruder

als Freymaurer und Mitglied unferer ☐, empfehlen
ihn als folchen zur brüderlichen Liebe und Vnterftützung.
im Orient zu Wien den Tag des Monats im Iahr des
Lichts 57

Ο ΚΑΝΩΝ
ΤΟΥ
ΠΟΛΥΚΛΕΙΤΟΥ.

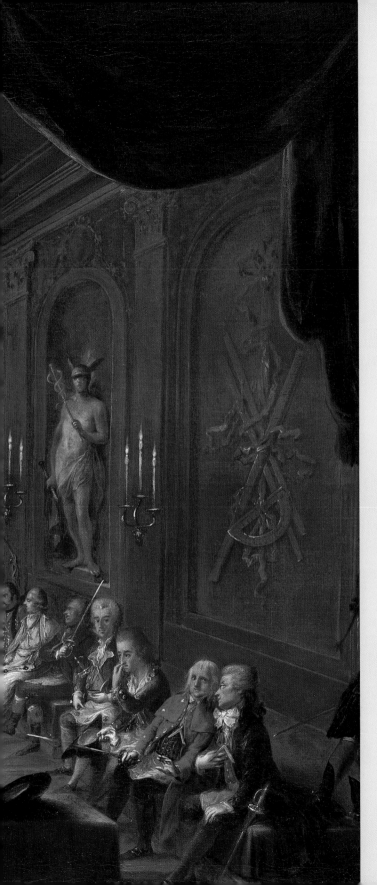

This painting, depicting an elaborate Masonic ceremony of initiation in Vienna in the 1780s, illustrates the importance that was attached to Masonic activity and the commitment required to do the work. As the picture suggests, participation in the Degrees is a moving experience that can provide much insight into one's self. The intellectual community was very much involved, and Mozart is said to be at the extreme right of this painting. It was common for swords to be used in early Continental initiations (see pp. 172–3). Freemasonry was also well-received in Scandinavian countries. The apron shown below is from Norway, where a different variant of Freemasonry – called the 'Swedish Rite' – evolved in the 18th century, and continues to be practised today (see pp. 212–13).

The American colonies proved an important breeding ground for Freemasonry, even after the Revolution. This early, printed American apron shows a large variety of Masonic symbols typical of aprons of the period.

The late 18th century saw the initiation of the first African Americans in the American colonies. This evolved into the Prince Hall Grand Lodge, named after the founder, Prince Hall, who had been initiated into an English military Lodge – Lodge No. 441 Irish Constitution, 38th Regiment of Foot, British Army – on 6 March, 1775. The movement spread and continues to flourish today. The photograph above of a Prince Hall Mason, dates to the 19th century.

THE
GRAND MYSTERY LAID OPEN;
OR THE
FREE-MASONS
Signs and Word difcovered.

All Secrets till they once are known,   But when once known we ceafe to wonder,
Are wonder'd at by every one,   Tis Equal then to fart or Thunder.

WHEN any Perfon is admitted a Member into this noble and Ancient Fraterni.y, He is inftructed to anfwer to the following Queftions, viz.

Howmany Signs has a true Free Mafon, Nine; which are diftinguifh'd intoSpiritual and Temporal. How many Temporal Signs are there ? Three. The firft is a Grip by the two firft Fingers, and is call'd Jachin and Boaz ; the fecond is a Grip by the Wrift, and call'd Gibboam and Gibberum; the third is a Grip by the Elbow, and is called Thimbulum and Timbulum. Have the fix Spiritual Signs any Names ? Yes, but are not divulged to any new admitted Member, becaufe they are Cabaliftical ? What are thefe Signs, The firft is Foot to Foot, the fecond is Knee to Knee, the third is Breaft to Breaft, the fourth is Hand to Back, the fifth is Cheek to Cheek, the fixth is Face to Face. Who is the Grand Mafter of all the Lodges in the World ? *I N R I.* What is the meaning of that Name ? Each diftinct Letter ftands for a whole Word, and is very myfterious. How is the Mafter of every particular Lodge called ? Oakechar-ing a Tocholochy.

By what Name are all the Members diftinguifh'd ? By the Name of Iftowlaw-leys. Who is your Founder ? God and the Square. What is God called ? Laylah Il-laliah, which is there is no other God but God. What is the Square call'd ? Whofly Powu Tigwawtubby which fignifies the Excellency of Excellencies. What pofture were you in when you receiv'd the fecret Word ? I fat on my Right Knee with the Holy Bible at my Breaft. Why do you hold the HolyBible at your Breaft ? for the EnjoyningSecrecy, and becaufe in it is con-tained the Grand Secret of Mafonry. Who was the firft Mafon ? Laylah Illallah. Who invented the fecret Word ? Checchehabed-din Jatmouny. What is it ? It is a Caba-liftical Word compofed of a Letter out of each of the Names of Laylah Illallah as mentioned in the Holy Bible.

Where fat King John in the Morning when he affembled the Society ? He fat in the Eaft Window of the Temple in a Chair of Marble waiting the rifing Sun. where fat He in the Evening when He dif-miffed it ? At the Weft End of the Temple in the fame Chair waiting the fetting Sun. Why was St. John called King ? Becaufe He was Head of all the Chriftian Lodges, and from his Superiour knowledge in the wonderfull Art of Mafonry. What are the Day and Night made for ? The Day is made for Man to fee in, the Night is made for Man to hear in. What is the moft uf-full Member ? The Ear, becaufe Men ought to hear more than they fpeak. What are the Tools requifite for a Free-Mafon ? The Hammer and Trowel, the one to feperate, the other to join. What Names are given to them ? Afphahani and Tala-gaica. By what Oath did you Swear to conceal the fecret Word ? By God, the Square, the King, and the Mafter. At the Inftallation of any Member the Perfon to be admited dreft with an Apron before Him, a Trowel in his right Hand, and a Hammer in his left, kneels on his right knee with a Bible on his Breaft, fupported by the Trowel, and in this Pofture He Swears to keep fecret the Word and Signs by which a Free-Mafon is known over all the World, the Privileges they enjoy by being admitted Members into this Ancient Society are very great, for a Member of any Lodge is oblig'd to Furnifh another Member tho' of a different Lodge, with all Neceffaries in his diftrefs and fupport Him to the utmoft of his Power.

Printed in the Year, 1726.

The public fascination with Freemasonry goes back to the very beginning of the Order's history, but grew when a member of the nobility – the Duke of Montagu – became Grand Master in 1721. This interest fuelled many exposés alleging to reveal the nature of Freemasonry, of which *The Grand Mystery Laid Open*, left, published in 1726, is an early example. Interestingly, about a third of the way down the left column is a comment stating that certain Masonic words are 'Cabalisttical' – perhaps an indication that the Order was thought to be associated with the Hermetic/ Cabbalistic tradition of the Renaissance. This could have been understood as a positive or negative idea, depending upon the reader.

The illustrations on the right are from a French exposure of a little later. It purports to show the signs and symbolic devices used in the various Degrees. There have been some studies that suggest that during this time a few 'exposures' which contained intentional misinformation were published by Masonic Lodges. Persons seeking admittance to Lodges using this material could then be identified and excluded.

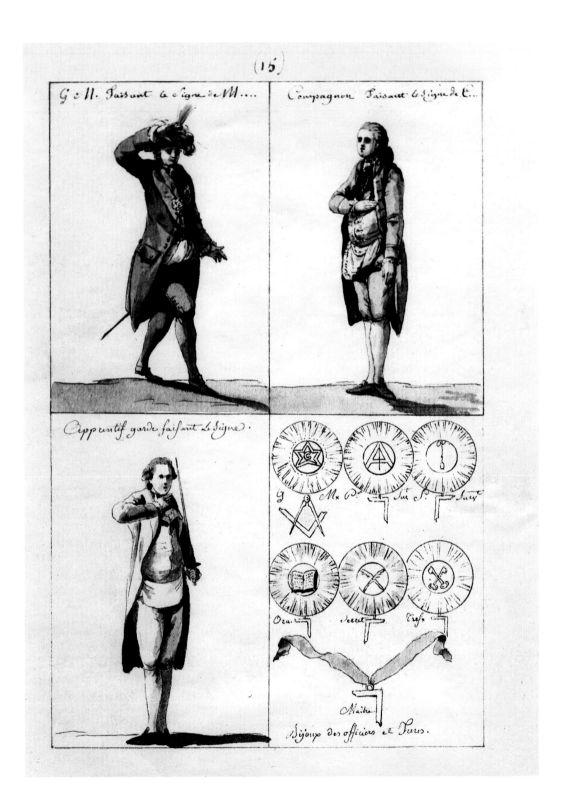

Pɪɪ

LES SECRETS,
DE
L'ORDRE
DES
FRANCS-MAÇONS,
Devoilés & mis au jour
PAR MONSIEUR P***
Nil eſt adeò abſconditum quod non tandem reveletur.
SECONDE PARTIE.

A AMSTERDAM
MDCCXLV.

The frontispiece of the exposure above, published in Amsterdam in 1745, purports to show part of the Third Degree ritual, while the title page contains various other symbols. While intending to expose Freemasonry's practices, it seems not to have been malicious. The frontispiece on the page opposite, from the French work *Les Francs-Maçons Ecrasés* (The Freemasons Destroyed) has a quite different connotation. The picture indicates the destruction of a Masonic Lodge and the distress of the Master. The destruction of Freemasonry was certainly the intent of some of those who wrote exposés, and that is why some of that work is as inaccurate as it is. Later material is generally more deliberately harmful (see pp. 248–51).

S. Fokke inv. et fec. 1746.

As the Order grew 'Higher Degrees' appeared, perhaps most numerous in France. In England the Holy Royal Arch Degree is thought to have developed in the 1740s. It was said to have been at the very heart of the Masonry practised by the Antient Grand Lodge. On the left is an early 19th-century Holy Royal Arch tracing board with a very important symbol, the Triple Tau, at the base of the pedestal.

On the right is an Irish apron of 18th-century beadwork. It shows many of the symbols of the Craft Degrees together with symbols of the Holy Royal Arch, such as the Ark of the Covenant, while the cockerel is a symbol of the Masonic Knights Templar. This Order was begun in the 18th century, in emulation of the medieval Knights Templar, and uses an exclusively Christian symbolism – the cockerel, for example, is a reference to Peter's denial of Christ (Matthew 26:34).

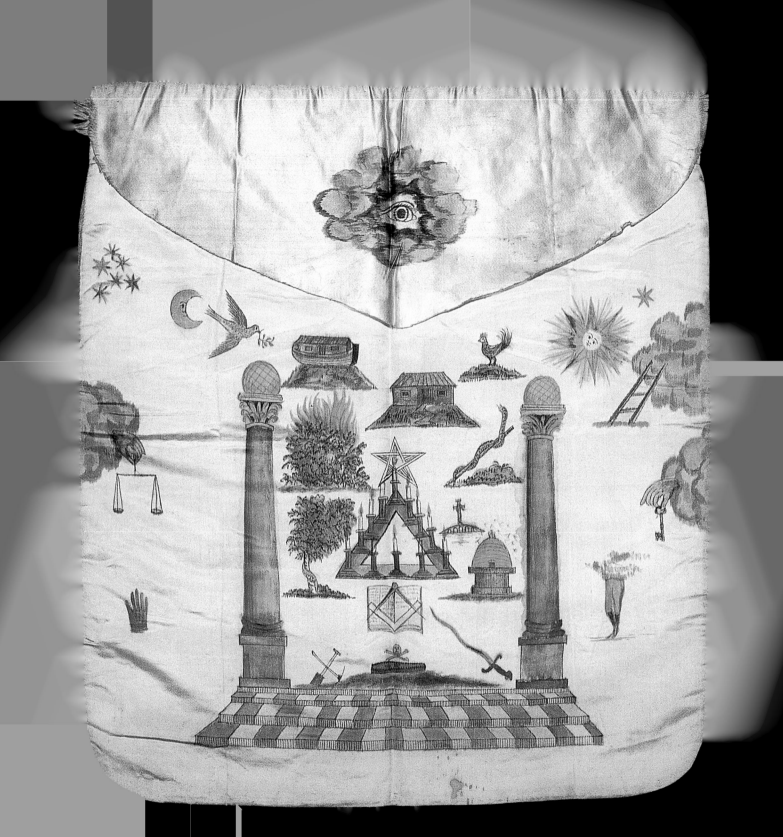

There is no international
standardization of Masonic
symbolism, making it difficult to
determine the Order to which the
apron opposite belongs. In the mid-
19th century individual Grand
Lodges began to specify which
symbols were to be present in
specific Degrees. Until that time
Brethren wore – or had made –
aprons that had Masonic symbols that
were pleasing to them. The symbols
on this apron, as on many others
shown here, relate to various
Orders. Most of the symbols are of
the Craft Degrees, but others – for
example, the Triangle with Candles
in the centre – relate to the Masonic
Knights Templar Order.

Higher Degrees have always been
popular in France. The Scottish Rite
(*Rite Ecossais*) originated there in
1758, originally having only 25
Degrees. During the 18th century
there were many Scottish Rite
Lodges in various American
locations, but the Order proper was
introduced to the United States –
where it is today perhaps most
popular – in Charleston, South
Carolina, in 1801. The drawing to
the right is the frontispiece to a
French work on the Scottish Rite.
There are a few symbols of the
Craft Degrees, bottom centre,
many symbols relating to Solomon's
Temple (for example, the 'Sea of
Bronze' supported by twelve oxen),
and a Templar Cross. Most of these
symbols relate more to the workings
in France than to those in the
United States.

The symbolism of these French watercolours alludes to
different Degrees within the early French *Rite Ecossais*. They
were probably done privately by an individual Brother for his
own use – to remind him of the principles taught, and to
enable him to recall the experience of receiving the Degree.
They are very specific, unlike the drawings that are used with
the lectures that are given as instruction in support of rituals.

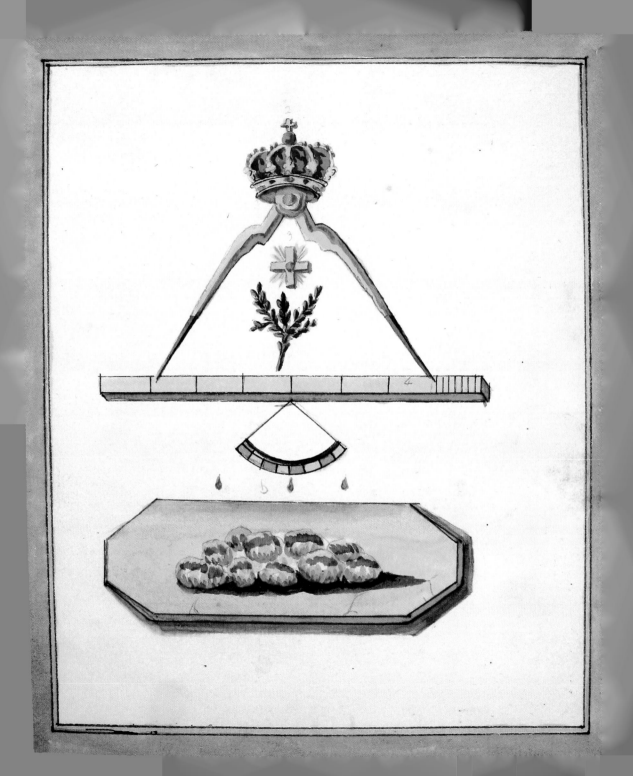

Condemnatio Societatis, feû Conventicularum -- *de Liberi Muratori* -- aùt -- *de Francs Maffons* -- fub pœna Excommunicationis ipfo facto incurrendæ, ejus abfolutione excepto Mortis Articulo Summi Pontifici refervata.

CLEMENS EPISCOPUS
SERVUS SERVORUM DEI.

Univerfis Chriftifidelibus falutem, & Apoftolicam Benedictionem

I N eminenti Apoftolatus Specula, meritis licèt imparibus, Divina difponente Clementia conftituti iuxtà creditum NobisPaftoralis providentiæ debitum jugi (quantum ex alto conceditur) folicitudinis ftudio iis intendimus, per quæ erroribus, vitiifque aditu interclufo, Orthodoxæ Religionis potiffimùm fervetur integritas, atque ab univerfo Catholico Orbe difficillimis hifce temporibus perturbationum pericula propellantur.

Sanè

On 28 April, 1738 Pope Clement XII issued a Bull (left) which forbade members of the Catholic faith to be Freemasons. The Bull made no statement of specific wrongdoing, and the reason for its publication is unclear. Perhaps the Church, which regarded itself as the only proper religious authority, was uncomfortable with its members being close with persons of other faiths.

Just a little later the Inquisition certainly took issue with Freemasonry, as highlighted by the story of John Coustos. Swiss-born but a naturalized British subject, he lived in Portugal in 1743 when he was elected Master of a Masonic Lodge meeting in a private house. The Inquisition learned of this and arrested him. He was interrogated for many days and finally condemned to the galleys. He was released at the request of the British ambassador and after agreeing never to speak of his experiences returned to London where he wrote a book – *The Unparalleled Sufferings of John Coustos* – illustrated with suitably gruesome images, as seen opposite. Happily this period has passed, and today Catholics are permitted to join the Order.

The relationship between Freemasonry and the Church has varied considerably from country to country. In France, for example, Freemasons were often accused of being anti-clerical. In England, however, until recently it was not at all unusual for Anglican priests also to be Freemasons, and many still are. The Masonic jewel worn by founding members of Abbey Lodge Westminster No. 2030 (right) demonstrates that there are Brethren with serious religious connections who see no conflict between Freemasonry and the Church. While not a religion, Freemasonry certainly draws upon religious history and philosophy – as seen in the depiction of a Jewish High Priest with his breastplate in the goblet opposite – and one often finds Hebrew inscriptions.

In general, it seems to be that those religions that feel they hold the only true faith and that other religions are false seem to be those that oppose Freemasonry. Certainly Freemasons are positively inclined toward religion, and many are very much so. The Volume of Sacred Law (in this case the Bible) which its binding tooled laboriously with Masonic symbolism is an indicator of the effort and commitment Masons are prepared to give to their religious affiliations.

Boitard.delin.   B.Cole sculp.et dedit.

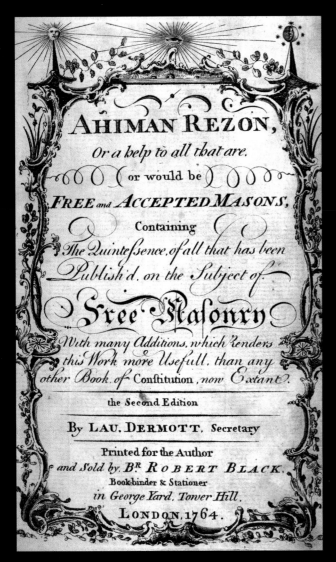

The Antient Grand Lodge was established in 1751, in opposition to the premier Grand Lodge, and the two English Grand Lodges competed for sixty-two years. The frontispiece of the *Constitutions* of the premier Grand Lodge – called the 'Moderns' by the Antients – published in 1767 is shown opposite. The image adopted by the Moderns in some way reflects the competition between the two organizations. Britannia sits looking serenely over London and the North Sea with the tools of the Craft and the Arms of the Moderns under her arm. The picture conveys the idea of a calm and well-established organization that has its place in society.

Ahiman Rezon (best translated as 'A Help to a Brother'), the constitution of the Antients, was first published in 1756; the title page and frontispiece of the 1764 edition are shown above. The frontispiece shows the arms of the Antients (top) and the arms of the Operative Craft (bottom). This conveys the idea that in the Antients one finds the traditions of both speculative and operative masonry which they claimed that the Moderns had abandoned.

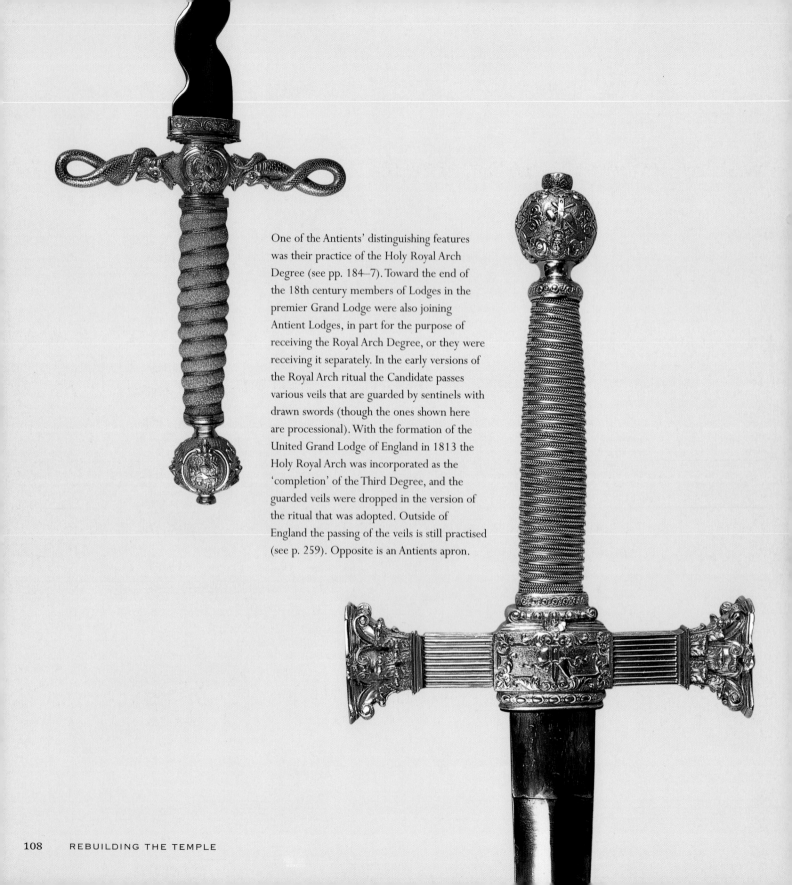

One of the Antients' distinguishing features was their practice of the Holy Royal Arch Degree (see pp. 184–7). Toward the end of the 18th century members of Lodges in the premier Grand Lodge were also joining Antient Lodges, in part for the purpose of receiving the Royal Arch Degree, or they were receiving it separately. In the early versions of the Royal Arch ritual the Candidate passes various veils that are guarded by sentinels with drawn swords (though the ones shown here are processional). With the formation of the United Grand Lodge of England in 1813 the Holy Royal Arch was incorporated as the 'completion' of the Third Degree, and the guarded veils were dropped in the version of the ritual that was adopted. Outside of England the passing of the veils is still practised (see p. 259). Opposite is an Antients apron.

HOLINESS TO THE LORD.

TO

RELIEF AND TRUTH

The arms of the premier Grand Lodge, which are adapted from the arms of the Operative Craft, are seen opposite with additional tools that can be associated with the Holy Royal Arch (see p. 274). In 1813 H.R.H. the Duke of Sussex became Grand Master of the Moderns and H.R.H. the Duke of Kent became Grand Master of the Antients. Under the influence of these two Royal brothers Articles of Union were agreed in six weeks, and the United Grand Lodge of England was formed on 27 December 1813. With union, the arms of the two Grand Lodges were impaled to create a new arms of the United Grand Lodge of England, shown above left. The arms of the premier Grand Lodge – the 'Moderns' – are found in the senior position, but the Antients gained certain concessions such as including the Holy Royal Arch Degree, signified by the Ark at the top. Previous mottos were dropped in favour of the words 'Audi Vide Tace' which provide an instruction to all members: 'Hear, See, Be Silent'. In 1919 the arms of the United Grand Lodge were again modified to include the Border of Lions (above, right) which reflects the longstanding association of Freemasonry with the Royal Family.

There is much romantic literature that seeks to portray Freemasonry as a revolutionary organization and as the causal factor in various revolutions. In terms of the American Revolution the division of public opinion was more accurately based on social class than of organizational membership. Among the wealthy American colonists there were more Tories, and among the less affluent there were more Whigs. There were Freemasons in both groups; and, as in most conflicts of that sort, there were Freemasons fighting on both sides. In the illustration on the left Masons who were on the side of the colonies and who were subsequently to become prominent in American society are shown with appropriate respect. To the right, one of those, Benjamin Franklin, is shown holding the key to the Bastille – presented to him by French Revolutionaries. But Franklin, himself, was not a militant revolutionary. Indeed, he was a critic of the Boston Tea Party.

This French print summarizes the principles of the Freemason's journey. At the lower right a man runs blindfolded from a cave that contains all the temptations of ordinary life. As he passes between the two columns, capped with the terrestrial and celestial spheres, he begins the Masonic journey. That journey is pictured as a path up the mountain, passing many trials and tests, and culminating at the summit illuminated by Divine light. On the pedestals at the sides are two groups of women depicting Law and Justice without Pity (left) and Mercy (right) – two conflicting principles that must be reconciled and applied. At the bottom of the column on the right are the words 'Au nom de l'Etre Supreme d'Ecosse'. This is a term for the Deity, apparently derived from the Scottish Rite. Intriguingly this print echoes the form of the large artificial mountain (and column) erected by Jacques-Louis David for the Festival of the Supreme Being, a pageant held on 8 June 1794. David was himself very likely a Freemason (see p. 285).

PRIÈRE M∴

Arbitre souverain de toutes choses, toi qui d'un regard embrasses l'espace, devant qui passent les mondes comme la feuille qu'emporte le vent, du haut de ton éternité entends nos vœux; éclaire-nous d'un rayon de ta divine lumière, embrase nos cœurs d'une étincelle de ton amour immense, nous serons les apôtres de ta loi, le monde nous comprendra, et ralliés au drapeau de la fraternité, tous les hommes marcheront harmonieusement dans la voie du progrès et de la perfectibilité.

LES CINQ ONCLES.

1. Napoléon Bonaparte (1er Consul et Empereur) Protecteur de l'Ordre des F∴M∴ né le 15 Août 1769.
2. Joseph Napoléon Bonaparte (Ex-Roi d'Espagne) Grand Maître de l'ordre des F∴M∴ né le 7 Janvier 1768.
3. Louis Napoléon Bonaparte (Ex-Roi d'Hollande) né le 1er Septembre 1778.
4. Jérôme Napoléon Bonaparte (Ex-Roi de Westphalie) né le 15 Décembre 1784.
5. Lucien Napoléon Bonaparte (Président du Conseil des Cinq-Cents) né en 1775.

Joseph Kiener R∴C∴, Editeur Place Maubert, 41.

This jewel design, captioned 'The Five Uncles', contains the images of Napoleon Bonaparte and his four brothers, Joseph, Louis, Jerome, and Lucien. The four brothers were all Freemasons, and two of them, Joseph and Louis, were appointed Joint Grand Masters of the Grand Orient of France by Napoleon in 1804, the year in which he declared himself to be Emperor. Although it has often been claimed that Napoleon himself was a Freemason, there is no evidence of his having been initiated in any specific Lodge. The Masonic Temple in Paris opposite, meanwhile, is believed to have housed the Lodge attended by Marat, Mirabeau and Robespierre, all important figures in the French Revolution.

A la G∴ du G∴

AU NOM ET SOUS LES AUSPICES DU G∴ O∴
DE FRANCE,

A∴ de L'U∴

IN THE NAME & UNDER THE AUSPICES OF
THE GRAND LODGE OF FRANCE,

A tous Maçons dispersés sur la surface du Globe,

Salut, Force, Union.

NOUS, VÉNÉRABLE ET OFFICIERS de la R∴ L∴ de St. Jean, sous le titre distinctif de La paix désirée, regulièrement en instance à L'O∴ de Wincanton, en Angleterre, et assemblés par les NN∴ M∴ connus des V∴ M∴ CERTIFIONS, que le T∴ C∴ F∴ Benjamin Plummer, agent commercial, ex-premier grand Serv. du G∴ O∴ d'angleterre, âgé de 39 ans, natif de Shepton-Mallet Dep.t Comté de Somerset, est membre de notre R∴ ATT∴ au troisième Grade symbolique, que la Régularité de sa conduite, ses bonnes mœurs et son exactitude aux Travaux, nous l'ont rendu cher et recommandable : Prions tous les Maçons réguliers, tant des OO∴ de France, que de ceux étrangers, de reconnaître ledit F∴ Plummer dans la dite qualité, de lui accorder la considération qui lui est due et de lui porter tous les secours dont il pourrait avoir besoin, comme nous aurions la satisfaction de le faire pour eux-mêmes.

EN FOI de quoi nous lui avons accordé le présent Certificat.

FAIT et DÉLIVRÉ en Loge, le 22.me J∴ du 9.me M∴ de l'an de la V∴ L∴ 5810 (ère vulgaire, le 22 Novembre 1810) signé de nous, contresigné de notre Secrétaire, et revêtu des Sceau et Timbre de notre Architecture, pour avoir son plein et entier effet, après la confrontation de la signature du dit F∴ qu'il a apposée devant nous.

To all Men enlightened on the surface of the Earth,

Greeting.

WE THE MASTER, WARDENS & MEMBERS of the Worshipful Lodge La Paix Désirée regularly assembled in the East of Wincanton, in England; DO HEREBY CERTIFY that our Worthy Brother Benjamin Plummer, commercial agent, late senior grand warden of the grand lodge of England aged 39 Years, born at Shepton-Mallet Dep. of County of Somerset, who has signed his Name in the Margin hereof, is a Master Mason in this our Lodge, of a good Report, beloved and esteemed amongst us: as such we earnestly recommend him to the brotherly Benevolence of all Free and Accepted Masons, & request them to protect and admit our said Brother Plummer into all Regular Lodges throughout the whole Universe, pledging a grateful return for the Kindness shewn to him.

IN TESTIMONY whereof we have hereunto subscribed our Names and affixed the Seal of our Lodge, this 22.nd Day of the 9.th Month A L∴ 5810 and November 22.nd A D∴ 1810.

Ne Varietur.

Vu par L'Orateur.

Le V∴

Le 2.nd Surv∴

Le 1.ier Surv∴

Scellé et Timbré par nous Garde
des sceau et timbre.

Par mandement de la R∴ L∴
Le secrétaire.

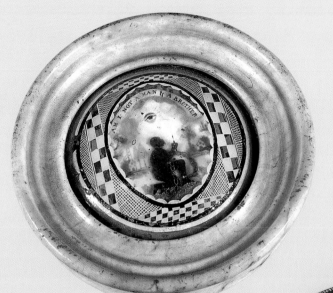

The years immediately after the French Revolution saw war in every corner of Europe as Napoleon expanded his Empire. The two works on this page were made by French soldiers while held prisoner by the English. It says something about the international nature of Freemasonry and the strength of fraternal spirit that they were allowed to form their own Lodges while in captivity – see the certificate opposite, written in English and French. For the prisoners, presumably it was important to them to meet regularly as Freemasons. The piece to the left recreates the anti-slavery medal made famous by Wedgewood in 1787, bearing the inscription 'Am I not a Man and a Brother?' – words with particular resonance for a Mason. The piece below includes most of the symbols of the Craft Degrees.

LODGE
OF
TRUE FRIENDSHIP
No. 1, BENGAL.

In the Name of God: Amen.

WE the Worshipful MASTER, WARDENS and SECRETARY of the LODGE TRUE FRIENDSHIP, No. 315, on the REGISTER of the GRAND LODGE of ENGLAND, and No. 1, Bengal: Do hereby CERTIFY that the Bearer hereof our well beloved BROTHER *John Fergusson Smith*

hath been lawfully entered an APPRENTICE, passed a FELLOW CRAFT, and raised to the SUBLIME DEGREE of MASTER MASON, and as such we recommend him to all MEN ENLIGHTENED, wheresoever spread on the Face of the GLOBE, that they treat HIM (after making TRIAL of his ABILITIES and comparing his Hand Writing with that on the margin,) with HOSPITALITY and Brotherly LOVE.

Given under our Hands and Seal at CALCUTTA, this *Seventeenth* day of *May* — in the year of our LORD One Thousand Eight Hundred and *Nine* and of MASON-RY 5809.

W. Dolby W. MASTER.
Th. Breton S. WARDEN.
Jas. Kilgour I. WARDEN.
Geo. G. Benjamin SECRETARY.

Au Nom de Dieu, Amen:

NOUS le Venerable MAÎTRE, Les SURVEILLANS et le SE-CRETAIRE de la LOGE TRUE FRIENDSHIP (ou LA VRAIE AMITIÉ) No. 315. sur le RÉGISTRE de la GRAND-LOGE D'ANGLETERRE, et No. 1, en BENGAL: Nous CERTIFIONS par ces Présentes que le Porteur de celle-ci notre bien-aimé FRÈRE nommé, *Jean Fergusson Smith*

A été légitimement reçu Apprenti, passé par le second GRADE, et a été élevé au SUBLIME GRADE du MAITRE-MAÇON, et C'est en cette qualité que nous Le recommandons à tous les HOMMES qui ont reçus la LUMIÉRE, en quelque lieu qu'ils soient disperses sur la Surface du GLOBE; afin que ceux-ci se comportent vers le dit FRÈRE, (apres avoir fait L'EPREUVE de son HABILITÉ, et comparé son Écrit à celui qui est à la MARGE) avec HOSPITALITÉ et AMITIÉ fraternelle.

Fait sous nos Mains et le Sceau de notre LOGE a CALCUTTA ce *Dix Septime* Jour de *Mai* — de L'Epoque CHRETIEN-NE, Mille Huit Cens *Neuf* et de la MAÇONNERIE 5809.

W. Dolby VENERABLE MAITRE.
Th. Breton 1re SURVEILLANT.
Jas. Kilgour 2e SURVEILLANT.
Geo. G. Benjamin SECRETAIRE.

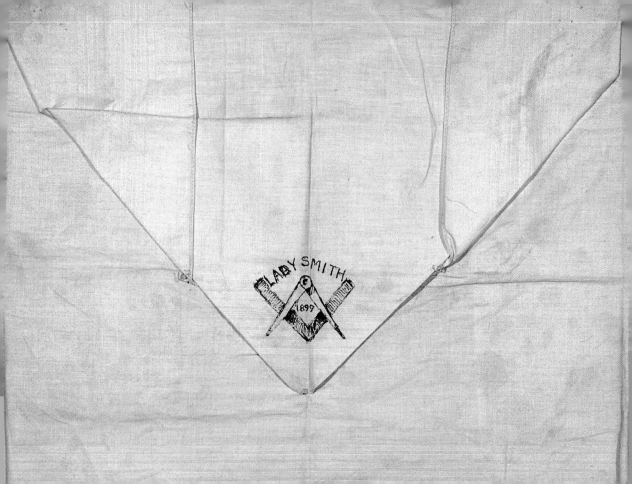

LORD KITCHENER LODGE
NO 3402 E.C.
MOASCAR EGYPT
1948

LAYING THE FOUNDATION-STONE OF THE NEW MASONIC TEMPLE AT SHANGHAI,—SEE PRECEDING PAGE.

Freemasonry in Africa, particularly in the English colonies, was conducted very much in accord with the rules of the parent Grand Lodge. The cornerstone laying ceremony opposite is being conducted in Lagos, at the time the capital of Nigeria. The regalia and the nature of the ceremony reflect the adherence of the Brethren to the practices of the United Grand Lodge of England. The print above, meanwhile, is in Shanghai where a similar ceremony is being conducted to lay the foundation stone of the Masonic Temple. The fact that it was appropriate to build a Temple there is an indication of the popularity of Freemasonry in China during the 19th century. The jewel to the right is one of those worn by founder members of Sierra Leone Holy Royal Arch Chapter. Much of the basic symbolism is traditional, but the arms at the centre of the jewel reflect the African essence of the Chapter.

The spread of Freemasonry to exotic, far-away lands was reciprocated by an analogous effect of foreign cultures on European Masonry. Freemason's Hall in Mainbridge, Boston, Lincolnshire, in England was built in 1860–63. The very careful reproduction of Egyptian columns and hieroglyphic symbols is an indication of the interest in that culture that had been started by the French incursion into Egypt under Napoleon. The Masonic certificate above, written in Italian and Arabic, was issued by the Italian-sponsored Grand Oriente d'Egitto.

Freemasonry was introduced into Latin America by a variety of Masonic organizations in Europe and the United States, and it has been very popular. The medal above left is from a Lodge in Uruguay, where the first Lodge, Asilio de la Virtud (Home of Virtue), was chartered by the Grand Lodge of Pennsylvania in 1832. The medal above centre is from a Lodge in Chile, where for the past seventy-five years Masons have worked to lift the condition of the Chilean people. The medal above right is from a Lodge in Brazil, where Freemasonry was established in Bahia in 1807. Early Brazilian Masons were intellectuals, and many clergy joined in spite of Church doctrines.

The Master Mason's apron opposite is from a Lodge in Venezuela. Lodges were chartered there by the Grand Orient of Spain in the early 1800s. In 1824 the Grand Lodge of Scotland formed a Provincial Grand Lodge in Venezuela and on 24 June of that year the Gran Logia de la República Bolivarina de Venesuela was founded. As in many European and Latin America countries, Freemasonry's private meetings caused concern in the government and Masonic activities were prohibited in Venezuela in 1827. The situation was resolved in 1838. Latin American Freemasonry has consistently promoted the principles of human rights, without being revolutionary.

In the 19th century Freemasonry was very fashionable, and it was common to find household items decorated with Masonic symbols. The blue and white pitcher and the coffee mug (below left) are decorated with a variety of such symbols which seem to be presented randomly rather that seeking to communicate instruction. It may be that the mug with the toad was offered to guests to encourage lightheartedness at the Festive Board. Both are English. The large blue and white cup below is typically Dutch.

The boxes opposite are each decorated with a general collection of Masonic symbols which seems to be as a sign of association with the Order. The snuff box (top right) is Swedish and was made in 1740. It has Masonic symbols on the top, while the pictures of Adam and Eve and the Tower of Babel on the sides seem to make reference to the idea of the very ancient origin of Masonry. The two wooden boxes are both 19th-century English and both are for general use. The Masonic symbols are set with mother of pearl inlay. The box in the bottom has much inlay of general decorative design with a collection Masonic symbols added in the centre-top. It appears that in some case fashionable, and popular, Masonic symbols were simply added to standard designs.

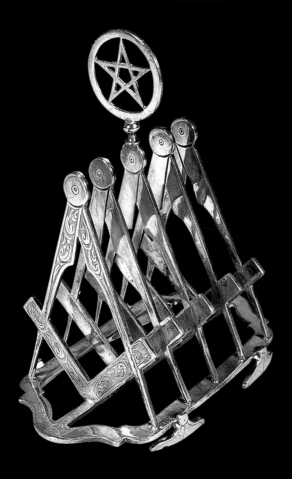

In the early 19th century Masonic images were very common in the decorative arts in the United States. The American quilt opposite was made in 1863, rather later than most. Such objects were usually made by members of the Order of Eastern Star (see pp. 234–5) or by members of a Freemason's family. Masonic images in the home were by no means limited to the United States. The Masonic toast rack above is English, and dates to the early 20th century, while the coffee pot is German and from the 1800s.

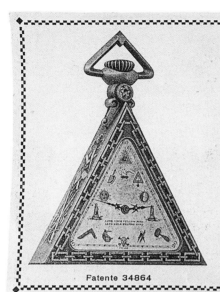

In the 19th century tobacco boxes were household items, and the example opposite has obvious Masonic connotations. Today the skull on the top would be considered a caution against smoking, but in the 19th century it was certainly a reference to the Mystical Death described in the ritual of the Third Degree. Some of the Masonic items of that period were quite personal. The Spanish advertisement for a watch with Masonic emblems in the positions of hours (above) and the similar watch, right, typify such personal objects. Since wrist watches have replaced pocket watches as the proper fashion, watches of triangular shape have become unusable.

The principal tenets of Freemasonry are Brotherly Love, Relief and Truth. It is important to practise them all in balance, but the final objective of the work is Truth. Over many years Masons in various parts of the world have placed emphasis of one of these tenets. The United Grand Lodge of England, opposite, is the source of Freemasonry and the centre of the English-speaking Craft. In general, English-speaking Masonry has focused on Brotherly Love in the form of good fellowship and social activity. That is no bad thing, but it is less than the Order's potential, and today in England and the United States there are movements to restore to the Craft a philosophical orientation. The Grand Orient of France, top left, has given much emphasis to the area of Relief, in the form of social reform. Many very valuable social benefits have resulted from their actions, though its involvement with politics and its interpretation of equality to admit atheists has caused the Grand Orient to be called 'irregular' by some Grand Lodges. In other parts of Europe, including Germany (above, the Lodge House and Museum at Bayreuth) and the Netherlands (left), the focus has very properly remained on Truth in the form of serious philosophical study.

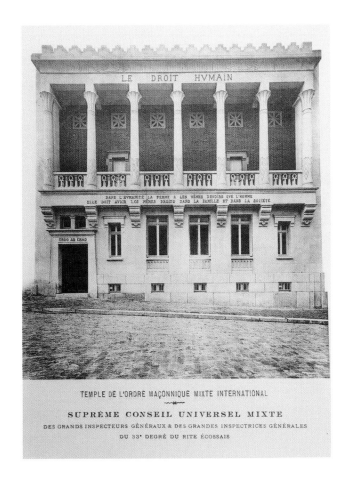

TEMPLE DE L'ORDRE MAÇONNIQUE MIXTE INTERNATIONAL

SUPRÊME CONSEIL UNIVERSEL MIXTE

DES GRANDS INSPECTEURS GÉNÉRAUX & DES GRANDES INSPECTRICES GÉNÉRALES
DU 33ᵉ DEGRÉ DU RITE ÉCOSSAIS

A sensitive issue has been the admission of women. Marie Deraismes, opposite, was initiated into Freemasonry in Loge Libre Penseurs of the Grande Loge Symbolique de France in 1879. It was a masculine Lodge, and her initiation set in motion the events that would result in the formation of 'Le Droit Humain', an international Order of androgynous Lodges. She later became *Grande Maitresse* of the Supreme Council of the Ancient and Accepted Scottish Rite established by the Grande Loge Symbolique Ecossaise Mixte de France. Dr George Martins, shown above with his wife, was a lawyer and Senator in Paris in the late 19th century; he was also a member of Freemasonry. Together with Deraismes he created the first Co-Masonic Lodge from which 'Le Droit Humain' grew. He was very interested in human rights, and it was through his efforts that 'Le Droit Humain' became an international Order, with its headquarters in Paris (above).

EMBLEMATIC CHART

MASONIC   HISTO

F. AND A. M.

G

CHAPTER No

COUNCIL COMMANDERY, ETC.

Advanced to the honorary degree of Mark Master   AD 18   AI 24
Presided as Master in the Chair   AD 18   AI 24
Received and Acknowledged a Most Excellent Master   AD 18   AI 24
Exalted to the most sublime degree of Royal Arch Mason AD 18   AI 24

CALLED FROM LABOR | TO REFRESHMENT
This   day of   AD 18   A.L. 58
Aged   Years   Months   days

HOLY BIBLE

TO ALL WHOM IT MAY CONCERN.

I do hereby Certify that

No   is a just and lawfully constituted
Lodge of Ancient, Free and Accepted Masons,
working under a Charter from the Most
Worshipful Grand Lodge of
In testimony whereof I set my
hand and affix the Seal of the
Grand Lodge this   day of

TO ALL FREE AND ACCEPTED MASONS.

We do hereby Certify that Brother
whose genuine signature appears on the margin hereof
has been regularly Initiated, Passed and Raised, and that
he is now a member of _____ Lodge No _____
located at _____
Distinguished for his virtues and fidelity to the
Craft, we recommend him to all Brothers and
Fellows, who are ever dispersed upon the Globe.
In testimony whereof we have hereunto
set our hands and affixed the Seal of our
Lodge this _____ day of _____
AD 18 _____ AL 58 _____

MASTER MASON'S RECORD.

Initiated as an Entered Apprentice _____ AD 18 _____ AL 58 _____
Passed to the degree of Fellow Craft _____ AD 18 _____ AL 58 _____
Raised to the Sublime degree of Master Mason _____ AD 18 _____ AL 58 _____

LODGE No.

3

The Making of a Mason

THE CRAFT DEGREES

*This certificate, dating from the
19th century, records the Lodge in
which the Brother received his
Degrees, and the dates on which
those Degrees were conferred.
Membership of a Craft Lodge is a
lifelong commitment: and when the
Brother is 'Called from Labor to
Refreshment', the date of his death
is recorded in the space above the
pedestal (bottom centre).*

THE THREE CRAFT DEGREES are at the heart of Freemasonry. Using elaborate rituals and lectures, they provide the Mason with the tools and knowledge necessary to work on his interior development, while the fraternal atmosphere of the Lodge provides a supportive environment. Once Initiated, Passed and Raised, the Brother is a Master Mason, and as with all other Master Masons, is eligible to occupy one of the Offices in the Lodge.

The first three Degrees of Freemasonry, those of the Entered Apprentice, the Fellow Craft and the Master Mason, are called the Craft Degrees and are the basis of the Masonic Order: together they encapsulate all of the essential teachings of Freemasonry. We do not know a great deal about the origin of these Degrees, and it appears that until 1717 each of the casual Lodges that were meeting throughout Britain (and perhaps in other countries) were using their own procedures and rituals. Most Lodges met in taverns or public houses, and it may be that most of the early proceedings consisted of readings and obligations made over dinner rather than the highly formalized ritual drama used today.

However, the various exposés that appear after the founding of the premier Grand Lodge suggest that some ritual may already have been in common use; and also that

As the Mason develops his understanding of Masonic symbolism he will come to understand that the Masonic Lodge can be interpreted as a representation of the human psyche. When considered in that context, the picture opposite of a 'Freemason Formed Out of the Materials of His Lodge' is a reasonable idea; and it is much more than the humorous image that it seems to be at first glance. The verse at the bottom reads: 'Behold a Master-Mason rare / Whose mystic portrait does declare / The Secrets of Freemasonry / Fair for all to read and see / But few there are to whom they're known / Tho' they so plainly here are shown.'

in the early years only two Degrees were worked. The Third Degree may have been conferred as early as the 1720s, but the first real evidence we have of the conferral of three Degrees is in Samuel Prichard's exposé *Masonry Dissected*, from 1730. While the premier Grand Lodge seems to have allowed Lodges to continue using their own variants of the ritual, there was some standardization, to enable Masons to identify themselves to each other, and the teachings were the same in principle. As Freemasonry developed during the early 18th century there seems to have been an increasing consistency in the practice of the various Lodges, and by the 1750s it seems that the Moderns and the Antients were practising generally similar rituals. The rituals and associated symbolic structure continued to evolve throughout the 18th century, with the major effort at standardization being William Preston's *Illustrations of Masonry*, first published in 1772.

In England the evolution of the ritual stopped in 1813 when the Lodge of Reconciliation, established to facilitate the unification of the Moderns and the Antients, demonstrated what is known today as the Emulation Working. Initially it was demonstrated, not published; and because of the difficulties of travel in the early 19th century, it was adopted very slowly. Even today there are many different 'workings' used by English Lodges, although their symbolic

SIT LUX . ET LUX . FUIT .

structure is consistent. North American Lodges used the rituals of the Grand Lodge from which they had received their Charter, until 1776 when the Lodges in the United States ceased to participate in the evolution of English ritual. Speaking very generally, Masons in the United States today use Antient ritual from the late 18th century with some updates from the work of Preston. Since there is a Grand Lodge in every State, there are sometimes noticeable differences.

Masonic Lodges in Europe, which started in the second quarter of the 18th century, began very quickly to develop their own ritual work; although because they were intended to teach the same lessons, the Degrees retained a basic similarity to the original English workings. However, the Degrees as worked in France, say, vary significantly from English counterparts.

As indicated earlier, it is the view of this book that the purpose of Freemasonry is to provide guidance for the mystical ascent that was the philosophical essence of the Renaissance, and the discussion of the symbolism of the various Degrees assumes this perspective. The interpretation of the symbols presented here is the personal view of the author, and is not endorsed by any Grand Lodge or Private Lodge. If Masonry

The painting opposite shows the major symbols of the Masonic Order, as well as many of the objects found in a Lodge. It provides an excellent visual aid for the instruction of the Brethren. The 'Lodge in a bottle' above is a British creation of the late 18th century, and shows a military Lodge meeting. During that period the placing of models in bottles was a popular, and very laborious, undertaking.

teaches the mystical ascent, then the Lodge and its symbols must be of a very personal nature. Sometimes Brethren refer to their Lodge as 'the Temple'; and we will do that, interpreting the word in the context of the Biblical question, 'Know ye not that ye are the Temple?'. We will look at the Lodge as a representation of the individual Mason, in particular that part of the individual which is today commonly called his 'psyche'. Of course, in 1717 no one thought of 'the psyche', but there is an abundance of literature of the time that indicates an intellectual interest in that level of consciousness. The idea that Masons might make a symbolic representation of it is not unreasonable.

Considering the Lodge as a representation of the psyche, we can also consider the Offices of the Lodge in this context. As we progress we will see that the Officers of the Lodge can be understood to represent various levels of consciousness, from the ordinary consciousness of the physical world, represented by the Inner Guard, to consciousness of the level of the Spirit represented by the Worshipful Master.

Finally, a psychological interpretation of Freemasonry allows us to consider the Three Degrees as three levels of consciousness within the psyche. The First Degree, the Entered Apprentice, represents the level of ordinary consciousness, that part of the psyche that interfaces with the physical world. The Second Degree, the Fellow Craft, represents the level that we might call the individual unconscious and the Soul. The Third Degree, the Master Mason, represents that level of consciousness that interfaces with the Spirit. These ideas will become clearer as we consider each Degree.

THE CRAFT LODGE

The term 'Lodge' refers as much to the group of men holding the Charter from a Grand Lodge as to the room in which they meet. Early Lodges met in private rooms in public houses; today Lodges meet in their own Lodge rooms, in Masonic Centres that offer facilities for a variety of different orders, or in one of the Lodge rooms in a Grand Lodge.

The room pictured here is the Lodge Hall of the Grand Lodge of Ireland, hung with portraits of former Grand Masters, but its plan is typical of every Lodge. The room is oriented in an East–West direction, with the Worshipful Master's station in the East (at the end of the room, with the celestial and terrestrial globes). Behind his chair is the Ionic Column, associated with the office of Master of the Lodge. The Junior Warden's station is in the South (right in this picture), and the Corinthian Column, associated with that office, is behind his chair. The Senior Warden's station is in the West, but in this picture his chair and his Doric Column are not visible. The benches are for the Brethren.

This is a guide to the objects found in a Craft Lodge.
While there are certain variations in Lodge layout in different
jurisdictions, this gives a good idea of the fundamental plan.
Examples of illustrations in this book of each object are given
in brackets.

1 **Ionic Column** (by Master's chair)
2 **Doric Column** (by Senior Warden's chair)
3 **Corinthian Column** (by Junior Warden's chair)
4 **Perfect Ashlar** (see p. 150)
5 **Rough Ashlar**
6 **Column with Celestial Globe** (see p. 150)
7 **Column with Terrestrial Globe** (see p. 150)
8 **Lights** (typical position, though they are sometimes found at
   three corners of the Chequered Pavement; these can be either
   candles or electric lights)
9 **Chequered Pavement**
10 **Blazing Star** (see p. 151)
11 **Tessellated Border**
12 **'G'** (suspended over the centre – see p. 123)
13 **Tassels** (see p. 230)
14 **Tripod and Lewis** (see p. 150)
15 **Point within Circle**
16 **Tracing Board** (see p. 161)
17 **Kneeling Rail**
18 **Kneeling Stool**
19 **Volume of Sacred Law, with Square and Compasses**
   (the Three Great Lights, placed on top of the pedestal)
20 **Volume of Sacred Law** (for Chaplain, for readings)
21 **Deacons' Wands**
22 **Stewards' Wands** (see p. 153)
23 **Warrant of Lodge** (on display)

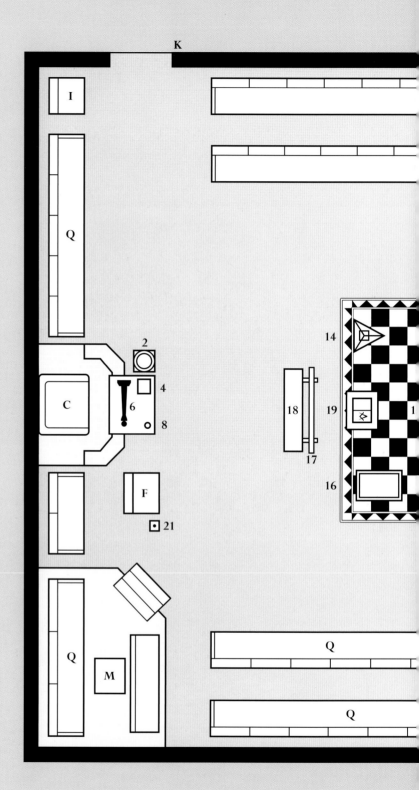

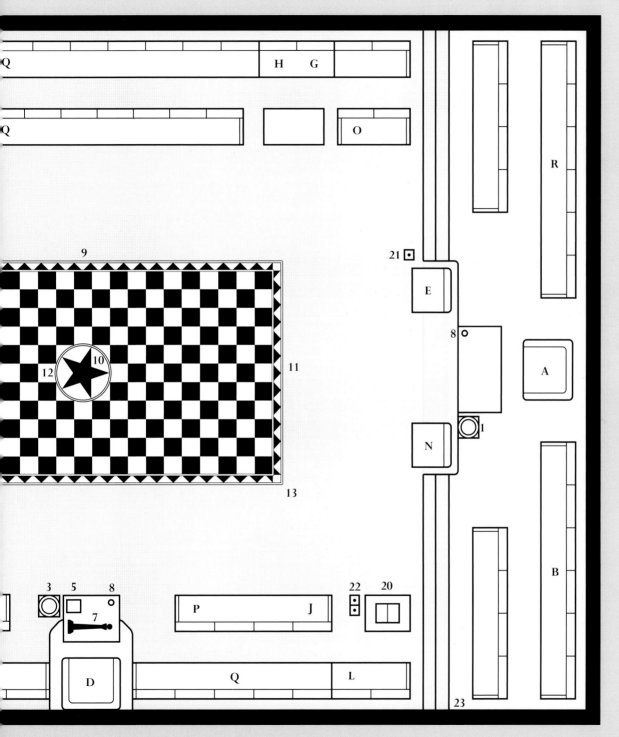

A   Worshipful Master

B   Past Masters

C   Senior Warden

D   Junior Warden

E   Senior Deacon

F   Junior Deacon

G   Secretary

H   Treasurer

I   Inner Guard

J   Steward

K   Tyler (stands outside
the Lodge)

L   Chaplain

M   Organist

N   Master of Ceremonies

O   Entered Apprentices

P   Fellow Crafts

Q   Master Masons

R   Visiting Worshipful
Masters

The Lodge room is orientated
around the points of the
compass, with the Master of
the Lodge sitting in the East.
Directions are important in
ritual work.

While the layout of a Lodge may vary a little, the objects found in every Lodge are fairly standard. The 'Lewis' is a metal device placed into a recess cut in a Perfect Ashlar. It permits the finished stone to be lowered into its place in the building in a way which would not be possible if the stone were wrapped with rope. In the speculative Craft the term 'Lewis' refers to the son of a Mason. The two columns, right, often topped with celestial and terrestrial spheres, are part of the equipment of the Wardens and they indicate the authority that those Officers have in the Lodge. Opposite is the ceiling in the Grand Lodge Hall of the United Grand Lodge of England. The Blazing Star of Glory is central in the starry heavens.

MASTER

The Worshipful Master presides in the East, and supervises the activities of the Lodge, particularly those of the Master Masons who were said to have met in King Solomon's Porch, the entrance to the Holy of Holies. This Office is best understood as a representation of that level of consciousness that relates to the Spirit in a manner analogous to the way the Ground Floor relates the physical world.

SENIOR WARDEN

The Senior Warden is said to be in charge of the 'Middle Chamber', a part of the Temple where the Fellow Craft plays a significant role. One can think of the 'Middle Chamber' as representing one's Soul, and certainly the symbols to be found there suggest that it is the seat of one's morality.

JUNIOR WARDEN

The Junior Warden is said to be in charge of the 'Ground Floor', the part of the Temple where the Entered Apprentice works. We think of the 'Ground Floor' as that level of ordinary consciousness which relates to the physical world. The Junior Warden can be understood to represent the 'Self' as the term is understood in Jungian psychology.

SENIOR DEACON

The Deacons are messengers. The Senior Deacon is the messenger of the Master, and he can be understood to be analogous to the capacity to be 'awake' and 'present in the moment'.

JUNIOR DEACON

The Junior Deacon is the messenger of the Senior Warden. In many respects he is analogous to the experience of 'feeling'. When one does the right thing one feels good; when one does the wrong thing one feels bad. One's feelings are an indication of how well one is following the principles of one's morality.

INNER GUARD

The Inner Guard is within the door of the Lodge and is the direct interface with the world outside. It is a good analogy for the Ego. Until the Ego forms an image of something, it is not admitted into one's consciousness. In an analogous manner, one does not enter a Lodge until the Inner Guard admits him.

TYLER

When we consider the Lodge as a model of the psyche, the Tyler, who is stationed outside the Lodge to exclude non-Masons and prevent eavesdropping, is rather like the central nervous system which is the interface between the physical world and the psyche, and is selective of the physical stimuli presented to consciousness.

A Lodge must be formed of a minimum of seven people, and there are seven essential offices, as shown opposite with their respective jewels of office. The jewel of the Steward of the Lodge is shown right, holding his wand. The Steward is not one of the Officers essential for the conduct of Lodge business, but many Brethren would consider him to be essential in other respects. He is responsible for the organization of the Festive Board held after Lodge and for other social activities.

The furniture of a Lodge can often be very elegant, and generally the chair of the Worshipful Master in the East will be the most elaborate, as can be seen here. In this picture the 'G' is of particular interest. The fact that it is attached to the Master's chair should not cause it to be associated with the Master. The 'G' is generally displayed in the East, and in some Lodge rooms there is not a convenient place to install it. Using the Master's chair as a platform can be a convenient way to display it properly.

The three ivory gavels below are assigned to the Principal Officers of the Lodge. That on the left is the Junior Warden's, that on the right is the Senior Warden's, that in the centre is the Worshipful Master's — they are identified by tiny carved capitals, and also by miniature versions of the Officers' jewels. Gavels are an important form of communication in the Lodge, used extensively in the rituals.

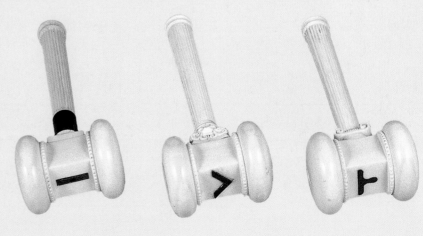

Fermeté.  *Courage.*

....

Le Profane   âgé

de   *né le*   *à*

Département de   *demeurant à*

Rue   *N.°*   *professant l'état*

a répondu aux questions suivantes :

Qu'est-ce que l'homme doit à Dieu ?

Que se doit-il à lui-même ?

Que doit-il à ses semblables ?

TESTAMENT.

O∴ DE CHALON-SUR-SAONE, des Presses du F∴ PILLOT.

The process of learning about one's self and making an interior ascent can be difficult, sometimes even distressing. No one should be persuaded to undertake such an activity; it should always be one's own wish to do so. For that reason no one is invited to be a Mason, one must ask to join the Order. The French petition for the Three Degrees, opposite, asks some questions about other requirements such as the need for the Candidate to believe in the Deity.

Instruction in the Lodge can happen in many different ways – perhaps through lectures, individual tuition, today even through contemporary audio-visual techniques. In the picture to the right Brethren are discussing the symbols of Freemasonry depicted on a tracing board. Such discussions are very valuable; one of the benefits of membership in a Lodge is being in a group within which such discussions can take place. And, as the picture suggests, they can result in some profound insights.

The symbols associated with Freemasonry are derived from many different sources, and all have specific and relative meanings. This plate shows almost all of the symbols associated with Craft Freemasonry, with basic meanings.

The Three Orders of Architecture, Ionic, Doric and Corinthian are the Pillars of Wisdom, Strength, and Beauty. They relate to the Principal Officers of the Lodge.

The Ladder rising from the **Volume of Sacred Law** indicates that the Divine instruction of one's faith is the only basis for such a journey.

The Level and the **Plumbrule** are the jewels of the Senior Warden and Junior Warden respectively.

Mason's grips reflect the Brotherly Love that unites the Brethren of the Order worldwide.

The Liferope can be seen as a symbol of Relief and Charity. Sometimes it is a cable in length and is used to measure distances.

The Gavel, the Chisel and **the Gauge** are the Working Tools of an Apprentice (see p. 164). By their use he will shape the **Rough Ashlar** that he is.

The Fellow Craft is the Second of the Masonic Degrees. His work is in the Middle Chamber of the Temple.

Ashlars are cut into various shapes to fit their functions in the building. These are very decorative.

The Temple. The purpose and the result of the building of the operative Craft.

The Operative Lodge. On every construction site of the operative Craft there was a Lodge, a small structure where the Craftsmen met, ate and did some types of work.

The Angel indicates the perpetual watchfulness of the Great Architect.

The Sprig of Acacia is a symbol of the never-failing hope of Divine guidance and protection.

The Masonic Lodge is a building in which the work of the Craft takes place.

The 47th Problem (or Proposition) of Euclid is a geometrical principle from the classical world. It is part of the basic understanding of right angles and thus fundamental to the craft of stonemasonry.

The Corinthian Capital is the most beautiful and most developed of the Three Orders of Architecture which the Mason should study and understand.

Building Stones carved with decorations that seem to have a classical source and are ready to be placed in the building.

The Keystone is an essential symbol of the Holy Royal Arch.

The Master Mason is the Third of the Masonic Degrees. His work is in King Solomon's Porch, the porchway entrance to the Holy of Holies.

The Perfect Ashlar is a stone ready to be placed in the building. It has been tested by, and can be used to test, the **Fellow Craft's tools**. It also represents the individual after he has worked to make himself better.

Arithmetic is one of the Seven Liberal Arts and Sciences which are recommended to the Fellow Craft for study.

Music is another of the Liberal Arts and Sciences.

The Triangle is not a symbol of Craft Freemasonry, but it is a Classical representation of the Deity – here shown appropriately in the Heavens.

The Chamber of Reflection opposite is a contemporary
reconstruction of a room which was originally used in the 18th
century. Before being admitted to the Lodge to receive the First
Degree the Candidate was asked to sit in the room, consider his
understanding of the work he was about to undertake, and write
his reasons for asking to become a Freemason. These were read
to the Brethren in the Lodge for their approval before the
Degree was conferred. The practice continues in some European
Grand Lodges, and is being revived in some American Lodges.
The French painting above illustrates some of the ideas on which
the Candidate might reflect. Although the situations are rather
extreme, the concept is not invalid. To undertake the mystical
ascent requires that one come to know one's self; and that can,
at times, be a difficult and stressful undertaking. A period of
reflection readies the Candidate for initiation.

The Jacob's Ladder is the ladder of consciousness by which one undertakes the mystical ascent. The three principal steps are Faith, Hope and Charity. Charity, the last step, is shown above.

The Rough Ashlar is a stone fresh from the quarry that must be cut to the appropriate shape before it can be placed in the building. It represents the Apprentice who has started his journey, and who must work to improve himself.

The Perfect Ashlar is a stone that has been cut and polished to its proper form and is ready to be placed in the building. It represents the Apprentice who has completed his work and is ready to advance to the Second Degree.

The Key was a symbol much used in the 18th century, but it has fallen out of use in recent years. It is the key to the Lodge, and it was said to be the Tongue by which the appropriate words establishing the identity of the Mason could be communicated.

Tracing boards are the basic training devices used to illustrate the material presented in the Masonic Degrees. The tracing board of the First Degree, opposite, illustrates many of the basic metaphysical principles of the Renaissance. It is said that God made the Universe, and Man, in his own image. The overall picture is of the Macrocosm, the entire Universe. The three columns, Wisdom, Strength and Beauty, communicate the idea of paired opposites, the blossoming Beauty of the Corinthian Column and the severe Strength of the Doric Column, held in balance by Wisdom, the Ionic Column. The ladder and the diagram on the pavement represent the Microcosm or Man. The Ladder stands between the Two Parallel Lines on the pavement. The Lines originally represented the Saints John whose days are mid-summer and mid-winter, paired opposites. The Ladder of consciousness between them holds them in balance. This is a Cabbalistic interpretation. In both the Macrocosm and the Microcosm there are four levels. The lowest of these is the physical world, symbolized in the Macrocosm by the Chequered Pavement and in the Microcosm by the theological virtue Faith. The second level up is that of the psyche which is represented in Macrocosm by the central area of the board with most of the symbols, and in the Microcosm by the theological virtue Hope. The third level up is the Spirit, represented by the Heavens and by the theological virtue Charity. The fourth level is Divinity. It is represented in the Heavens by the Star that contains the 'All-Seeing Eye' of the Deity; and It, the Source of all things, is the fourth level and the Source of both the Macrocosm and the Microcosm.

The floor cloth opposite illustrates the principal symbols of
Freemasonry, and would have been used in the First Degree
ritual. It was made in Germany in 1760, and it provides an
insight into how much the teachings of Freemasonry had
developed by that time and also how consistent the teachings are
among the several Grand Lodges. The French print above shows
a Lodge assembled for the initiation of an Entered Apprentice
Mason, using a similar floor cloth. The Candidate is shown with
his hand on the Volume of Sacred Law and is about to take his
Obligation as an Apprentice. The print certainly captures the
'feeling' of the ceremony, though it should be noted that many
of the postures and gestures shown here are not used in the
ceremonies practised in all jurisdictions.

The working tools of the Apprentice – the Gavel, the Chisel and the Gauge – are tools of action. The tools are introduced during the ritual, and displayed when discussing their symbolic meanings – there are three tools specific to each Degree. Applying these First Degree tools to one's self, one can think of the Gavel as representing passion, the capacity to introduce energy into a situation. The Chisel, which is said to represent 'education', can be seen to represent the capacity for classification and analysis which balances passion. The Gauge, which is 24 inches in length, can be understood to represent the intellectual capacity to determine how much of each of the other tools to use; and, since there are 24 hours in the day, when they should be applied. Opposite capabilities can thus be held in balance.

Once he has been initiated into the fraternity, the Entered Apprentice is presented with a certificate. The 19th-century certificate from the Grand Lodge Alpina of Switzerland, opposite, records the date upon which the Candidate received his Entered Apprentice Degree; the dates of subsequent Degrees, when conferred, are recorded so that the Candidate has a history of his experience.

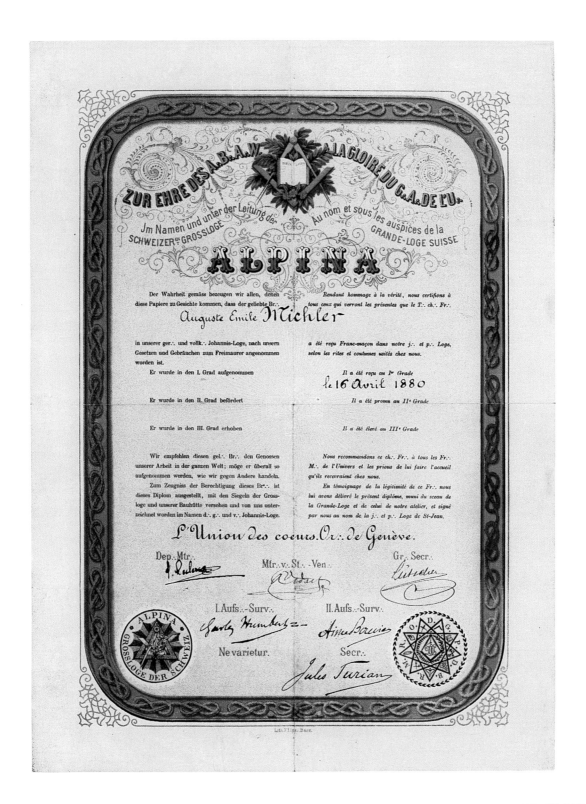

THE SECOND DEGREE

The Ear of Corn was, in the ancient world, considered to be a source of wisdom and enlightenment, and was included in various initiation rituals. Here we can understand it to represent a process of natural maturation of which the mystical ascent is part.

The Middle Chamber is guarded by the Senior Warden. It can be understood to represent one's Soul, the seat of one's morality. The Hebrew letter in the Middle Chamber is usually represented by the letter 'G', and it is a neo-Platonic representation of the Divinity.

The tracing board of the Second Degree opposite illustrates the task to be accomplished by the Fellow Craft. It is, in fact, a detailed drawing of part of the First Degree board. Of what part? Of the Microcosm, or of Man. The two columns are paired opposites because they are topped with the celestial and terrestrial spheres, and the Ladder between them has become a Staircase. The structure is a representation of Solomon's Temple, but we can understand it in the context of the question in the Great Light, the Bible, 'Know ye not that ye are the Temple?'. It is a picture of the Candidate, and the climbing of the Stairs is a representation of the start of the mystical ascent. The Middle Chamber at the top of the Stairs is the place where the Fellow Craft conducts most of his work.

The Junior Warden guards the bottom of the stairs. The password he asks for indicates that to climb these stairs one needs to have accomplished all the prerequisite tasks and one must have the proper motive.

The All-Seeing Eye is here, as it is in the First Degree tracing board; but here, as one starts one's interior ascent, it is more prominent, more personal. One's decisions are of great importance, and have a much quicker effect on one's experience.

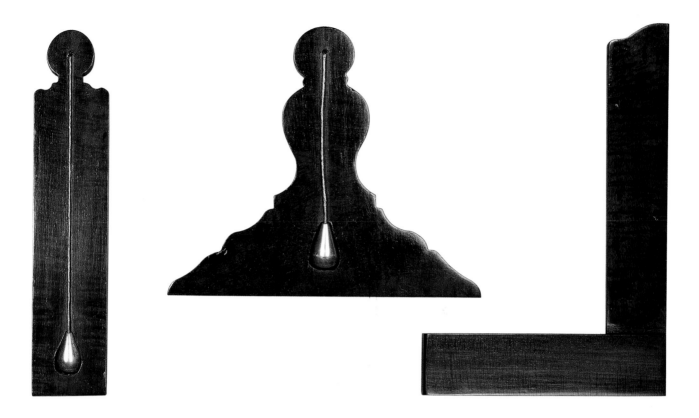

The Letter 'G', opposite, is considered by many Masons to refer to God, as this illustration suggests. But such a reference would, at face value, make no sense at all to a French Mason working in a Lodge in Paris. Some rituals say that the 'G' refers to Geometry, the fifth of the Seven Liberal Arts and Sciences, and describe it as a 'regular progression of science, from a point to a line, from a line to a superficies, from a superficies to a solid'. The first reference to this is in the exposure *Masonry Dissected*, 1730; in the response, *A Defence of Masonry*, 1730, the author refers us to 'Proclus in Euclid'. In that reference, Proclus says that a point moving generates a line, a line moving in a direction not parallel to itself, generates a superficies, and a superficies moving in the same way generates a solid. Thus the stuff of the point is the fabric of the line, the stuff of the line is the fabric of the superficies, and the stuff of the superficies is the fabric of the solid. Since Proclus was the last of the classical neo-Platonists, and the reference is in a work that is among the literature of the Renaissance Hermetic/Cabbalistic tradition, one is led to think that the Letter 'G' is a neo-Platonic reference to the Deity.

The three tools above are those of the Fellow Craft. Unlike the tools of action that belong to the Apprentice, these are tools of testing; each tests against an absolute criterion, two of which are opposites, and the third of which defines the relationship between the two. We can understand the Plumbrule (left) to relate to the use of 'licence'. In contrast, the Level (centre) relates to 'restraint'. The Square (right) defines the proper relationship between the two. In this way we can see that these Working Tools represent the individual's capacity for practising morality.

When one regards the tracing board as a symbol of a life at a level far short of its potential then the Sprig of Acacia is a sign of that life, a vegetable life. But it is a living thing, and it can be encouraged to grow.

If one contemplates seriously in one's Middle Chamber, sooner or later one is led to the Holy of Holies in the Temple that one is; and finding the door open, one is conscious of the Divine Presence. But when one is conscious of the presence of an unlimited Being, one's Self dies.

The tracing board of the Third Degree, opposite, makes reference to the process by which one becomes a Master Mason. It is a ritual in which all Master Masons participate, but it symbolizes an event which very few people actually experience in fact. Clearly, the idea of Death is of great importance; but from the perspective we are taking in this writing, that event described is quite different from the way death is usually understood. One of the interpretations of the idea might be that since the Fall of Man our lives are 'like death' when compared with how they were when mankind lived in Eden and was conscious of the Divine Presence. The death envisioned by the Master Mason's Degree is a process by which one can regain that consciousness. It is not a physical death, but rather the death of one's concept of one's Self. Perhaps the most insightful comment on the subject has been made by W. L. Wilmshurst: 'Hence the Third Degree is that of mystical death, of which bodily death is taken as figurative…. In all the Mystery-systems of the past will be found this degree of mystical death as an outstanding and essential feature prior to the final stage of perfection or regeneration'.

The Self which dies is the essential concept of one's being as one lives in the physical world, the level of the First Degree. The enacting of the ritual death is accomplished with the Setting Maul. Then one is raised to the level of the Spirit.

West is at the top of the tracing board of the Third Degree, occupying the place of East on the First Degree board. This indicates that the Master Mason has completed his journey to the East in search of knowledge, and now returns – to the West – to assist others with their journeys.

These 18th-century French drawings depict important parts of the Third Degree ritual. Although the ritual dramas of the Masonic Degrees teach the same lessons in every jurisdiction, the detail of the ceremonies can vary quite considerably from country to country.

The first scene in the sequence is top left: the Candidate for the Master Mason's Degree is received in the same ceremonial manner as in the preceding Degrees. Dignity and the intent of communicating instruction is the characteristic of the Masonic rituals. The next step, in the image below, is the 'death' of the Candidate. Although the Candidate experiences the ritual death, the ceremony is not conducted in a violent manner. In this drawing (below, left) the Candidate is being laid gently on to the floor cloth of the Third Degree.

In the next image, top right, a Candidate who has participated in part of the Third Degree ritual, is lying in a symbolic grave (to the left of the picture, covered in a sheet) while a second Candidate is being received. As the Degree progresses, both will be Raised at the same time. The ritual process of raising the Candidate from the symbolic grave (below right) communicates much Masonic information. It is actually a symbolic representation of his being raised from his previous psychological level of consciousness to consciousness at the level of the Spirit. When such a thing happens, in fact, it occurs entirely within the individual.

In the scene opposite, the Brethren point drawn swords at the Candidate. The practice seems to have developed in the 18th century when all French gentlemen carried swords, and is continued, with foils, in some Continental Lodges today. It does not intend to imply a threat.

Plan de la Loge du Maitre

The 'Plan of the Lodge of a Master' opposite gives a summary image of the role of the Third Degree in the mystical ascent. It is much more than a simple representation of the process of death as it is usually understood. The footprints describe the steps that the Candidate takes from the level of the psyche, symbolized by the Square, past the Death of the Self, symbolized by the Grave, to the level of the Spirit, symbolized by the Compasses.

The Working Tools of a Master Mason are the Pencil, the Skirret, and the Compasses. These are tools of Design. The Pencil is the active tool with which the drawing is accomplished, and represents creativity. The Skirret, a string on a reel, is a constraint on the pencil. It represents an understanding of the fundamental Laws by which we should restrain our creativity. The Compasses are an instrument of proportion; and as with the third tool in the other sets, the Compasses serve to keep the use of the other tools in balance.

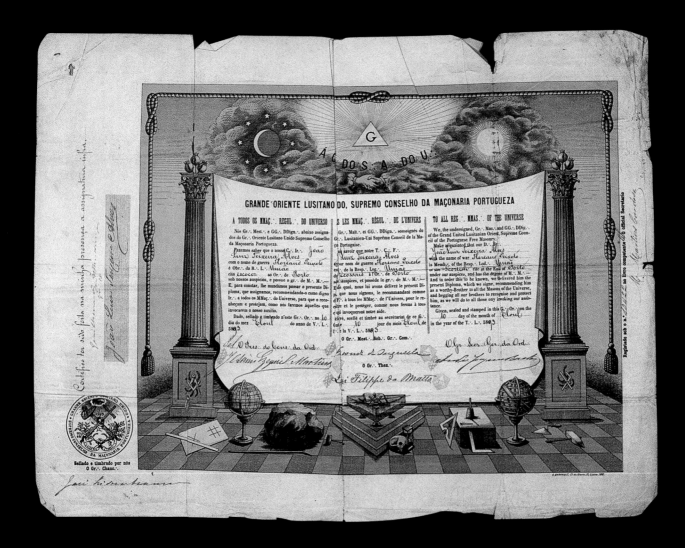

Upon the completion of the Third Degree the Candidate is
a Master Mason, and is entitled to participate in all Masonic
activities. The Lodge that confers the Degree typically presents
the newly raised Master Mason with a certificate, and some
of them are quiet elaborate. Both the Portuguese and French
certificates opposite and above record the conferring of each
of the Three Degrees.

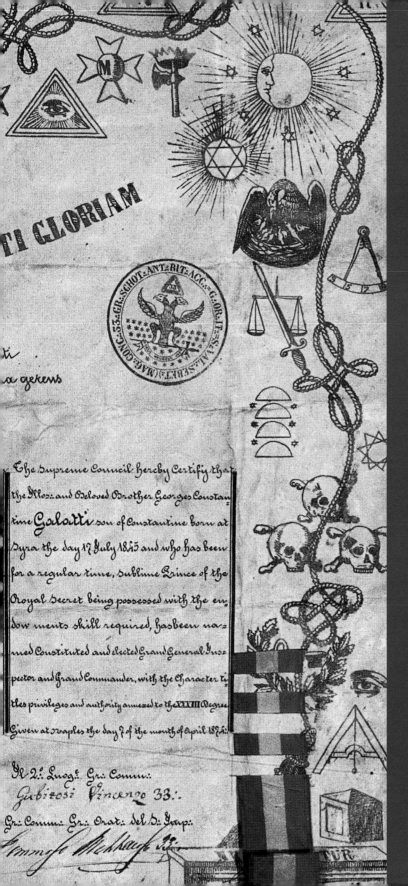

4

The Freemason's Path

HIGHER DEGREES

*As Freemasonry expanded in the
18th century many additional
Degrees were invented throughout
Europe. Today, the highest Degree in
Freemasonry is generally considered
to be the 33rd Degree of the Scottish
Rite, an honorary Degree which
is given only to those Brethren
who have provided great service
to the Rite. The Italian certificate
shown here is from c. 1870, and it
commemorates the elevation of a
Brother to that honorary status.*

U PON COMPLETING the Third Degree, the new Master Mason is eligible to participate in many other Masonic organizations. These new Rites and Orders, often referred to collectively as the 'Higher Degrees', offer more detailed interpretations of various Masonic teachings, and by participating in them a Brother is able to develop specific interests.

The origins and history of the Higher Degrees are as much of a puzzle as the origins of Freemasonry itself. Shortly after the founding of the premier Grand Lodge additional Degrees were being practised by Lodges in some areas, and since there were no regulations about the structure of Freemasonry in the early 18th century, Lodges practised Degrees and rituals that they found to be attractive. Over the years a faint pattern emerged, and there seem to be two groups of Higher Degrees – those that originated and prospered in Britain (including the Mark and Holy Royal Arch Degrees) and those that developed in France and on the Continent (including the Scottish Rite). However, these Degrees tended to mutate and switch territories quickly, leading to plenty of cross-fertilization. In his *Masonic Encyclopedia* Henry Coil lists over one thousand Higher Degrees, including such arcane creations as the Ancient and Primitive Rite of Memphis-Misraim, with 97 Degrees; here we will focus on the more prominent.

The origin of the British group of Degrees is unknown, but it may be that while the Craft Degree rituals evolved in England in the 18th century, parts of the Degrees were removed and pre-served as separate 'Side Degrees' by Brethren who thought they

The apron opposite is of Spanish origin, probably from the late 19th century, and is an apron of one of the Elu Degrees in the Scottish Rite. This Rite has thirty-three Degrees, each with their own regalia.

were important but who wanted to streamline the Three Degree system. The Mark Degrees provide an example of this. In the operative craft a craftsman would cut his 'mark' into the stones on which he was working. It identified the work done by each mason and enabled him to receive appropriate rewards. Each mason's mark was exclusively his and was received when his apprenticeship was complete. The Mark Degrees, which emphasize that each of our actions is identified and associated with us, seem originally to have been part of the Fellow Craft Degree. When (and if) they were separated from that Degree is not clear, but records of the conferral of the Mark Degrees first appear in the 1760s. In England today they are administered by a separate Grand Lodge in London which has taken other similar Degrees, such as Royal Ark Mariner, under its wing and manages them also.

Just as the Mark Degree can be seen as the completion of the Fellow Craft Degree, so too has the Holy Royal Arch Degree been seen as the completion of the Master's Degree. This Degree, which has a more Christian flavour, was practised enthusiastically by the Antient Grand Lodge (see p. 108), and later by Brethren of the premier Grand Lodge who observed it separately from their Masonic activities. Today it remains widely practised in England, where Royal Arch Chapters are attached to Craft Lodges.

The 'Continental' group of Higher Degrees is centred on the *Hautes Grades* that emerged in France in the 1740s. These

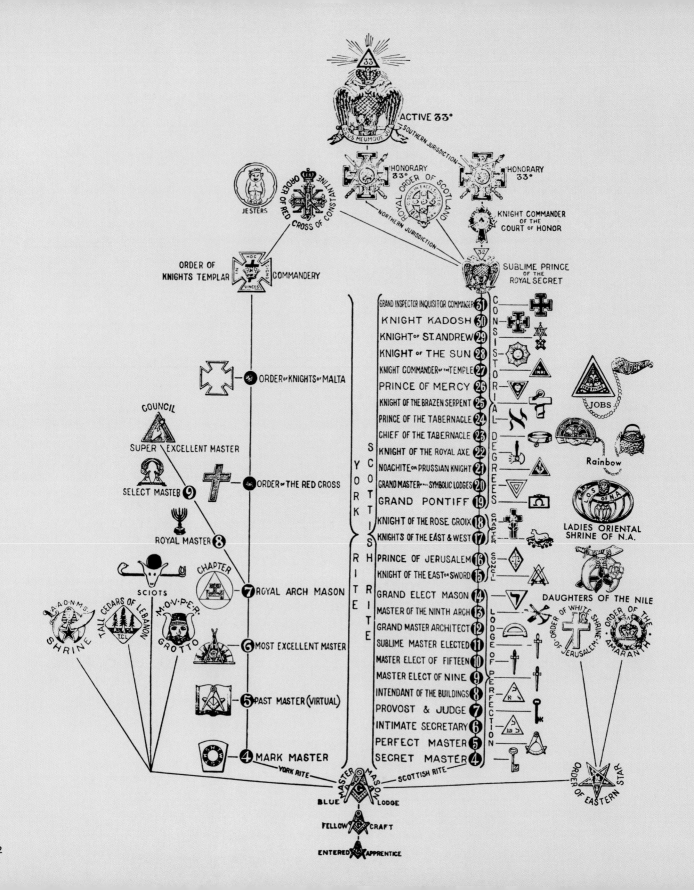

ACTIVE 33°

SOUTHERN JURISDICTION

JESTERS

ORDER OF RED CROSS OF CONSTANTINE

HONORARY 33° ORDER OF SCOTLAND

ROYAL ORDER OF SCOTLAND

NORTHERN JURISDICTION

HONORARY 33°

KNIGHT COMMANDER OF THE COURT OF HONOR

ORDER OF KNIGHTS TEMPLAR — COMMANDERY

SUBLIME PRINCE OF THE ROYAL SECRET

GRAND INSPECTOR INQUISITOR COMMANDER **31**

KNIGHT KADOSH **30**

KNIGHT OF ST. ANDREW **29**

KNIGHT OF THE SUN **28**

KNIGHT COMMANDER OF THE TEMPLE **27**

PRINCE OF MERCY **26**

KNIGHT OF THE BRAZEN SERPENT **25**

PRINCE OF THE TABERNACLE **24**

CHIEF OF THE TABERNACLE **23**

KNIGHT OF THE ROYAL AXE **22**

NOACHITE OR PRUSSIAN KNIGHT **21**

GRAND MASTER OF ALL SYMBOLIC LODGES **20**

GRAND PONTIFF **19**

KNIGHT OF THE ROSE CROIX **18**

KNIGHTS OF THE EAST & WEST **17**

PRINCE OF JERUSALEM **16**

KNIGHT OF THE EAST OR SWORD **15**

GRAND ELECT MASON **14**

MASTER OF THE NINTH ARCH **13**

GRAND MASTER ARCHITECT **12**

SUBLIME MASTER ELECTED **11**

MASTER ELECT OF FIFTEEN **10**

MASTER ELECT OF NINE **9**

INTENDANT OF THE BUILDINGS **8**

PROVOST & JUDGE **7**

INTIMATE SECRETARY **6**

PERFECT MASTER **5**

SECRET MASTER **4**

CONSISTORIAL DEGREES

CHAPTER

COUNCIL

LODGE OF PERFECTION

SCOTTISH RITE

YORK RITE

ORDER OF KNIGHTS OF MALTA

COUNCIL

SUPER EXCELLENT MASTER

SELECT MASTER **9**

ORDER OF THE RED CROSS

ROYAL MASTER **8**

CHAPTER

SCIOTS

ROYAL ARCH MASON **7**

A.A.O.N.M.S. SHRINE

TALL CEDARS OF LEBANON T.C.L.

M.O.V.P.E.R. GROTTO

MOST EXCELLENT MASTER **6**

PAST MASTER (VIRTUAL) **5**

MARK MASTER **4**

YORK RITE

JOBS

Rainbow

L.O.S. OF N.A.

LADIES ORIENTAL SHRINE OF N.A.

DAUGHTERS OF THE NILE

ORDER OF WHITE SHRINE OF JERUSALEM

ORDER OF THE AMARANTH

MASTER MASON

BLUE LODGE

SCOTTISH RITE

ORDER OF EASTERN STAR

FELLOW CRAFT

ENTERED APPRENTICE

182

Degrees embraced a variety of idioms such as Chivalric Legends, the Classical Mysteries, the building of the Second Temple, and Biblical events such as the Flood and Noah's Ark. In the Degrees relating to the Second Temple important underground vaults were said to have been found by Scottish Masons, and from this came the term *Rite Ecossais*, or 'Scottish Rite'. It should be noted that these *Hautes Grades* were very soon as popular in the rest of Europe as they were in France and more Orders were produced throughout the 18th century. In Sweden a whole separate Masonic system emerged, influenced in part by the German Chivalric Rite of Strict Observance (see pp. 212–13).

One particularly important evolution from the *Hautes Grades* in France was the Order of Knights Templar. Widely practised in Britain and the United States, the Templar Rites seem to have had their origins in the 'Kadosh Degree', a Degree in the *Rite Ecossais* which relates to activities of the Knights Templar in the medieval period, and which first appeared in Lyons in the 1740s. The Order probably found its way to Britain in the 1750s where it became associated with the Holy Royal Arch. It is thus a fascinating example of crossfertilization between the two systems of Higher Degrees.

The Higher Degrees today find their clearest expression in the United States, where there are essentially two paths open to the Master Mason: the York Rite, or the Scottish Rite. The York Rite is a codification of the 'British' school of Degrees, though placed in the 'correct' order: Mark, Holy Royal Arch, then Royal and Select Masters and Knights Templar. The Royal and Select Masters Degrees originated in Britain, but were taken up more enthusiastically in the United States, and were then exported back to Europe.

The alternative system, the Scottish Rite (as practised in the United States), dates in its present form to 1801. However, it had been introduced to the United States in 1761 by Etienne Morin, who had received a Patent authorizing him to form a Lodge to confer twenty-five of the Higher Degrees of the *Rite Ecossais*. Today there are Supreme Councils of the Ancient and Accepted Scottish Rite for the Northern and Southern Jurisdictions which are located in Lexington, Mass., and Washington, D.C. respectively. They confer thirty-two Degrees and an honorary 33rd Degree. Finally, we must not forget the various other associated organizations open to Master Masons, some of which are very popular. These include Shriners, the Order of the Secret Monitor and the Masonic Rosicrucians. Each has its own special interpretation of the teachings of Freemasonry, and each offers the Master Mason further opportunities for expanding his knowledge.

The diagram opposite describes the Higher Degrees and related organizations in the United States. Similar, though by no means identical, relationships exist throughout the world. The 92nd Degree collar above is from the Ancient and Primitive Rite of Masonry. This Rite can be traced to the Rites of Memphis and Misraim which were founded in France in 1813. Although the Ancient and Primitive Rite is practised today throughout the world, it is not recognized as a 'regular' Masonic Body.

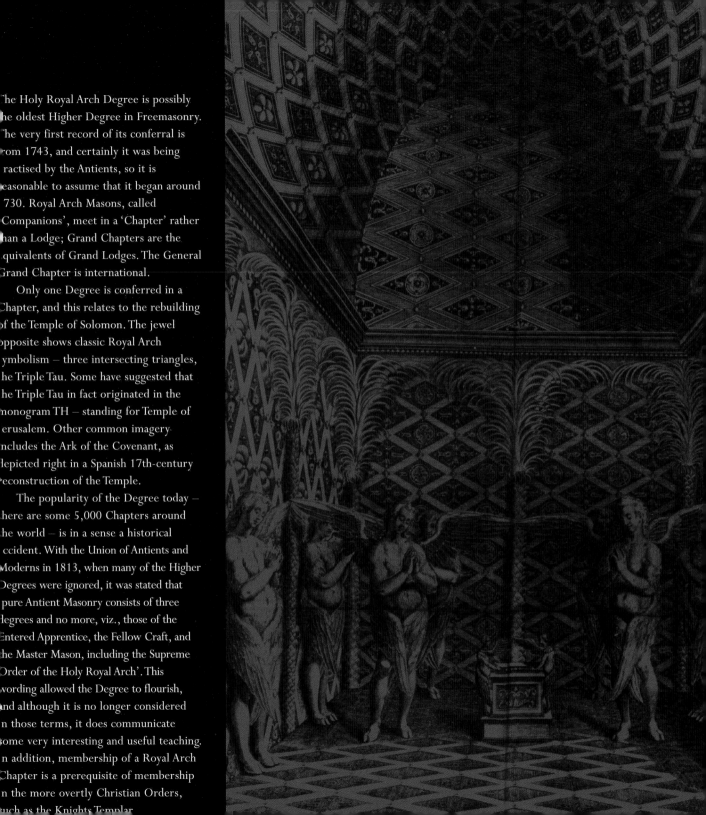

The Holy Royal Arch Degree is possibly the oldest Higher Degree in Freemasonry. The very first record of its conferral is from 1743, and certainly it was being practised by the Antients, so it is reasonable to assume that it began around 1730. Royal Arch Masons, called 'Companions', meet in a 'Chapter' rather than a Lodge; Grand Chapters are the equivalents of Grand Lodges. The General Grand Chapter is international.

Only one Degree is conferred in a Chapter, and this relates to the rebuilding of the Temple of Solomon. The jewel opposite shows classic Royal Arch symbolism – three intersecting triangles, the Triple Tau. Some have suggested that the Triple Tau in fact originated in the monogram TH – standing for Temple of Jerusalem. Other common imagery includes the Ark of the Covenant, as depicted right in a Spanish 17th-century reconstruction of the Temple.

The popularity of the Degree today – there are some 5,000 Chapters around the world – is in a sense a historical accident. With the Union of Antients and Moderns in 1813, when many of the Higher Degrees were ignored, it was stated that 'pure Antient Masonry consists of three degrees and no more, viz., those of the Entered Apprentice, the Fellow Craft, and the Master Mason, including the Supreme Order of the Holy Royal Arch'. This wording allowed the Degree to flourish, and although it is no longer considered in those terms, it does communicate some very interesting and useful teaching. In addition, membership of a Royal Arch Chapter is a prerequisite of membership in the more overtly Christian Orders, such as the Knights Templar.

The Holy Royal Arch focuses on the rebuilding of Solomon's Temple. In the process a crypt is discovered under the ruins of the Temple, as illustrated above. The crypt is in pristine condition, and had not been damaged in the Temple's destruction. Viewed from the perspective that 'ye are the Temple', the ruin can be understood as a human individual after the Fall of Man; but the pristine crypt indicates that within each individual is still a pure place where one can experience the Divine Presence.

The tracing board of the Holy Royal Arch, opposite, contains a few symbols of the Craft Degrees, but generally the symbols are archetypal images from the World of the Spirit, such as the Ox, the Lion, the Eagle, and the Man – images of the residents of the Four Worlds and the banners of the Twelve Tribes of Israel representing the twelve archetypal human types. They are represented by the signs of the zodiac in the crypt above.

MARK MASONRY

The Mark Degrees are of British origin, and have no connection with the Hautes Grades of the Continent. The first reference to them appears in Scotland, and they were also conferred in Lodges in England, Ireland and the American Colonies. At the formation of the United Grand Lodge of England the Mark Degrees were not included, and today they are administered separately. The Degree teaches that every one of our acts is notes and recorded, and that we are rewarded for them. This is emphasized in the Mark tracing board, below, in which at the lower left a Mark Mason presents his mark at a Wicket to receive his wages. Symbols of Craft and Mark Degrees appear together, indicating the closeness of the two Orders.

Regalia in Mark Lodges is limited to an apron and jewel. The jewel above, which is from the early 19th century, is that of the Senior Warden of a Mark Masons Lodge. Opposite is a more modern Mark jewel (with the same monogram in Hebrew), and an early Mark apron from Albany Lodge, Isle of Wight, showing the keystone and the tools associated with the Mark Degrees: the Mallet and Chisel. Note also the Triple Tau on the bottom of the Keystone. Iconographically there is a great connection between Mark and Holy Royal Arch – this is made more explicit in the York Rite, where both Degrees are worked in a Chapter.

176

ALBANY LODGE
NEWPORT .I.W.

Royal Ark Mariner Lodges are administered by the Grand Lodge of Mark Master Masons in several countries, though there is no connection between the workings. The teachings of the Degree are derived from the Biblical legend of the Deluge, and that event and its difficulties are used to represent the hazards of our own lives. Emphasis is given to the providence and mercy of the Deity, to the promise of salvation, and to the need to practise the Cardinal Virtues. The instruction points out that the chaos caused by the Deluge, while disastrous, was not the end of all things; and we, working together and facing the reality of our situations, can rise above the difficulties that we encounter. The importance of the family, the need for each individual to work in such a way as to provide benefit for all, and the importance of assisting those less fortunate, are also emphasized.

equipping of a 'Secret Vault' or 'Crypt' in Solomon's Temple and c
background for the Holy Royal Arch, which involves the rediscove
that vault. The four Degrees worked are the Select Master, the Ro
Master, the Most Excellent Master (this is sometimes omitted), ar
Super Excellent Master. The drawing below illustrates part of the
Masters Degree which deals with the vessels for the Holy Temple
design typifies the 'cryptic' qualities of the Degrees in the Cryptic

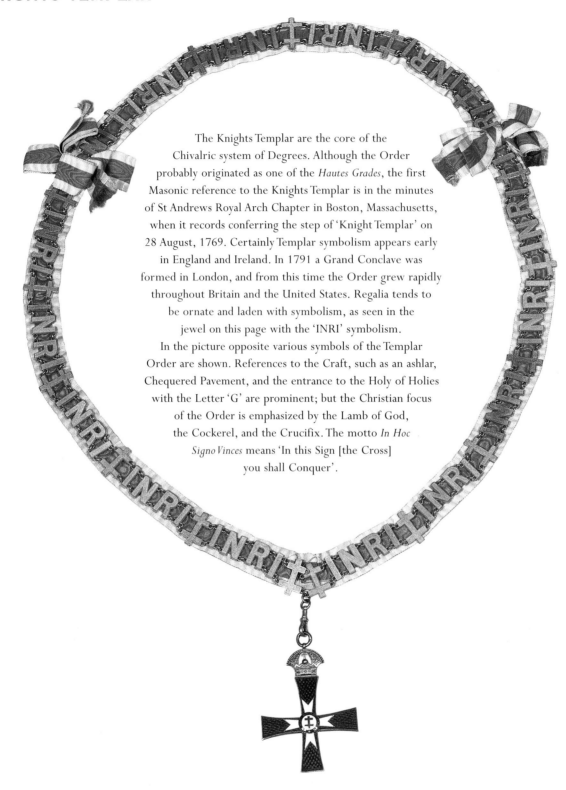

The Knights Templar are the core of the
Chivalric system of Degrees. Although the Order
probably originated as one of the *Hautes Grades*, the first
Masonic reference to the Knights Templar is in the minutes
of St Andrews Royal Arch Chapter in Boston, Massachusetts,
when it records conferring the step of 'Knight Templar' on
28 August, 1769. Certainly Templar symbolism appears early
in England and Ireland. In 1791 a Grand Conclave was
formed in London, and from this time the Order grew rapidly
throughout Britain and the United States. Regalia tends to
be ornate and laden with symbolism, as seen in the
jewel on this page with the 'INRI' symbolism.

In the picture opposite various symbols of the Templar
Order are shown. References to the Craft, such as an ashlar,
Chequered Pavement, and the entrance to the Holy of Holies
with the Letter 'G' are prominent; but the Christian focus
of the Order is emphasized by the Lamb of God,
the Cockerel, and the Crucifix. The motto *In Hoc
Signo Vinces* means 'In this Sign [the Cross]
you shall Conquer'.

The chapel opposite is the Knights Templar Chapel in Dublin, and it shows clearly the Christian nature of the Order. The lessons communicated by the Templar ritual and practised by the Knights are typically Christian: Brotherly Love, Truth, Charity, Hospitality, and Universal Benevolence.

Above is a Commandery (the Templar equivalent of a Lodge), set up for ritual. As with the Craft Degrees, rituals vary around the world. Initially in the United States a single Degree was conferred in a Commandery. Now, as in other jurisdictions, three Degrees are conferred: The Order of the Red Cross, The Orders of the Mediterranean Pass or Knights of Malta, and The Orders of the Temple. These Degrees have different names in different places, but all are Christian in their content and very moving for Christian Masons.

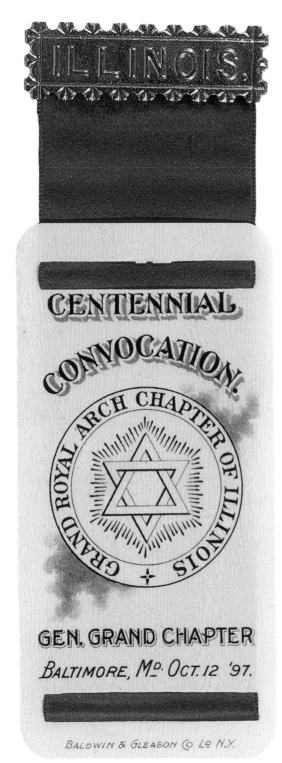

The York Rite could, in fact, very well be called the American Rite. Essentially it is a codification and rationalization of the 'British' Higher Degrees discussed on pp. 184–95, placed into a consecutive order that implies progression. In fact the York Rite is made up of three distinct jurisdictions: Chapters, Councils and Commanderies (as shown on p. 182). The first confer the Mark and Royal Arch Degrees; the second confer the Royal and Select Masters Degrees; and the third the Chivalric Degrees.

The material on this page relates to the first jurisdiction, the Chapter. The first recorded Chapter was in Fredericksburg Lodge, Virginia, in 1753. The first General Grand Chapter was formed in 1797 (as commemorated by the badge left), and in this respect the United States was ahead of England, where there was no overall governing body for Royal Arch until 1813. The Keystone on the medal right, above is a distinctive symbol of the Holy Royal Arch, as are the interlaced equilateral triangles. Opposite is the certificate of a Chapter of the Holy Royal Arch. It serves the same purposes as that of the Craft Lodge certificates. It depicts the Mason being lowered into the preserved Crypt (see p. 187), to retrieve something that was lost.

There is a Grand Chapter in each State, corresponding to each Grand Lodge, and the General Grand Chapter of Royal Arch Masons International is the largest Masonic Body in the world, since unlike the Craft Degrees, it cuts across national boundaries.

After the Chapter, the other two bodies in the York Rite are the Council and the Commandery. The distinctive triangular jewel above is that of a Grand Council of Royal and Select Masters. That body governs all the Councils of Cryptic Masons within a particular state – in this case, Ohio. Grand Councils of each State operate under the General Grand Council International.

The Knights Templar apron opposite is also triangular, which is typical of early 19th-century American regalia for this Order. The Skull and Cross Bones together with the Coffin admonish one to 'remember death', the Crossed Swords part of the qualities of a Knight, the Hour Glass reminds us that our time is running out, and the Lamb of God and the Cockerel point out the Christian duties.

THE SCOTTISH RITE

The Scottish Rite did not originate in Scotland but in France. While originally it probably had twenty-five Degrees, today it has thirty-three, of which the first three are more or less the same as the Craft Degrees, and are usually conferred in a Craft Lodge. There is a ritual for each degree, though the extent to which they are worked varies from jurisdiction to jurisdiction. In France, for example, it is possible to work from the First to the 33rd in the same Lodge. However, in the United States groups will attend theatrical performances of the degrees, after which it is conferred. In the UK the first degree to be worked is the 18th, the Knight of the Rose Croix – and for this reason Scottish Rite Masonry in England is often known as 'Rose Croix' Masonry. In England, all degrees after the Rose Croix Degree are by invitation only, while the 33rd Degree everywhere is honorary, and is rarely awarded.

The event depicted in the photograph here is dedication of the Albert Pike Memorial in Washington D.C. conducted in 1901 – exactly one hundred years after The Supreme Council, 33rd Degree, Ancient & Accepted Scottish Rite was founded in Charleston, South Carolina. Albert Pike was a remarkable individual. He was born in Massachusetts and travelled to many places in the South and West of the United States as a teacher, journalist and lawyer, as well as a Justice of the Supreme Court of the State of Arkansas. He was initiated into Freemasonry in 1850, and joined the Scottish Rite in 1853, soon becoming an influential member. He understood the mystical background of Freemasonry, and participated in the rewriting of all Scottish Rite Degrees. It is generally acknowledged that Pike deserves the credit for the successful organization and growth of the Scottish Rite. His works, particularly *Morals and Dogma*, contain valuable teachings and still read and are highly regarded today.

The range of material covered by the Scottish Rite is immense, as indicated by these Degree arms. The arms top left are of the Second Degree, the Fellow Craft, which is now conferred in Craft Lodges. The symbols are similar to the ones which we have seen in connection with that Degree. Above are the arms for the 13th Degree, the Master of the Ninth Arch. The 'cryptic' context of the Degree is clear; and as we have seen, this Degree of the *Rite Ecossais* may have been the origin of the Cryptic Degrees (see p. 191). To the left are the arms of the 30th Degree, the Knight Kadosh. The Degree requires an affirmation of faith, warns of the usurpation of power by authorities, and encourages one to assume responsibility for one's self. It was quite possibly this Degree that led to the Knights Templar Order in Britain. Opposite are the arms of the 33rd Degree. This is the highest Degree in the Ancient and Accepted Scottish Rite, and it is conferred only on those Brethren who have given great service to the Order. Note that these drawings are European – symbols may be somewhat different in other parts of the world.

SAPIENTIA

DEUS MEUMQUE JUS

J.T. LOTH. DEL.   IMP. MONROCQ. PARIS.

The Brother, opposite, is wearing the uniform of a Knight Kadosh, the 30th Degree. The sword, the cloak with a Cross, the Knight's hat and the boots all relate the the chivalric aspect of the Degree, although the style is not of the medieval Templar period when the Degree ritual is set. The photograph is from the 19th century, when it was not uncommon for Brethren to be seen in regalia.

In the engravings on this page, Brethren of the Scottish Rite are shown wearing traditional regalia and standing in postures associated with the various Degrees. Along the top, starting at the left: 4th Degree (Secret Master); 14th Degree (Perfection); 18th Degree (Rose Croix); 30th Degree (Knight Kadosh); and right, 32nd Degree (Prince of the Royal Secret); 33rd Degree (Grand Inspector General). This unusual work was a gift, sent in 1815 from Brussels to the Dutch royal city of The Hague.

The collar opposite is for the 32nd Degree of the Scottish Rite. The Double-Headed Eagle is a symbol of the Degree, and also of the Scottish Rite as a whole; the other symbols include the Encampment associated with the 32nd Degree and the Crosses of the Degrees that relate to the Templars.

Although there are ritual dramas associated with each Degree, the task of conferring thirty-two Degrees on each Candidate is very time consuming. Therefore, in general in the United States, the Degrees are conferred on a 'Class'. One Brother participates as the Candidate while the others in the Class observe the Degree, which has the quality of a theatrical production, and commit themselves to the appropriate obligations. The drawing above is a design by the Great Western Stage Equipment Co. of the setting for Cyrus's Treasury, and the set was installed in the Scottish Rite Temple in Kansas City, in 1952.

Aside from the Scottish and York Rites, there are other
Masonic organizations that can offer a great deal. The red Fez
and the jewel opposite are regalia of the Ancient Arabic Order
of the Nobles of the Mystic Shrine. Founded in 1872, the
Shrine has Temples throughout North America and Mexico.
It is frequently thought of as an organization that participates
in parades, but for more than eighty years its principal activity
has been the care of crippled children. Today there are
nineteen hospitals providing orthopedic care and three burn
centres throughout the United States. They provide treatment
at no charge for children under eighteen.

The black Fez is part of the regalia of the Mystic Order of
Veiled Prophets of the Enchanted Realm, more easily known
as 'Grotto', founded in 1889. It is not thought of as a Degree,
rather it is an organization of Masons whose members meet
for good fun conducted in a proper fashion, and they have
serious charitable commitments, specifically funding
research into Cerebral Palsy and dental care for children
with special needs.

To the right is a jewel of the Order of the Secret Monitor.
This Order is based on the friendship between David and
Jonathan (Samuel 20) to teach the value of Brotherly Love and
true friendship. Its origins seem to have been in a similar
Order founded in the Netherlands in the 17th century. In
England it is a separate Order available to Masons. In America
it is conferred by the Allied Masonic Degrees.

The jewel left belongs to the Allied Masonic Degrees, an organization founded in the 19th century to preserve Degrees which are not at the present time associated with any Masonic body, but which are relevant to Masonic teachings. Some of them were at one time conferred as 'Side Degrees'; others were originally practised by the Antients, but were not included at the time of the Union. As well as preserving these Degrees, the organization encourages study and research. The apron below belongs to the Degree of St Lawrence, whose martyrdom is remembered by the symbol of the gridiron.

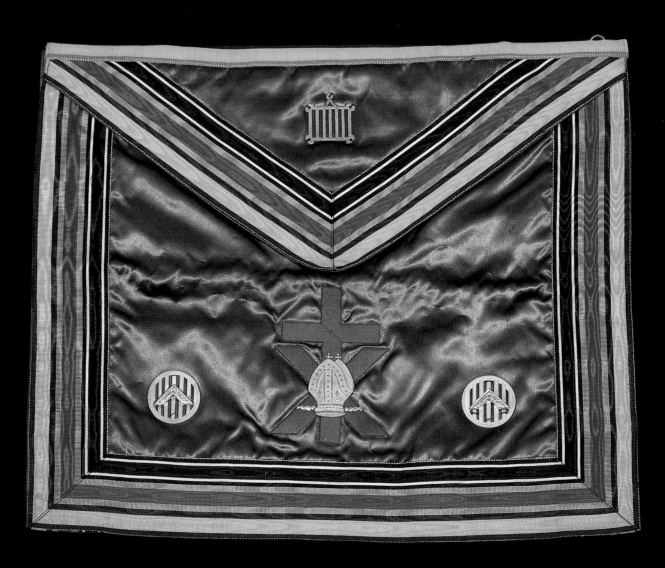

The three jewels above belong to the Societas Rosicruciana – those on the left and right are English (Societas Rosicruciana in Anglia), the one in the centre is American (Societas Rosicruciana in Civitatibus Foederatis). It is an invitational Christian Masonic society open to Master Masons which studies the material associated with the original Rosicrucian writings of the early 17th century (see p. 71), including the Hermetic/Cabbalistic tradition. Members of the Society (called *fratres*, Latin for 'brothers') progress through a series of nine grades – from 'Zelator' to 'Magus' – each having its own impressive and colourful ritual, in three distinct Orders. The jewel right is that of a 'Setter-Erector', a grade in an organization called 'The Worshipful Society of Free Masons, Rough Masons, Wallers, Slaters, Paviors, Plaisterers, and Bricklayers'. It is an organization of Master Masons, sometimes called 'The Operatives', that works to preserve the practices of operative masonry as they were worked prior to speculative Masonry.

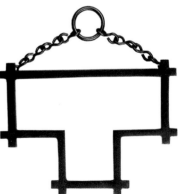

The Swedish Rite of Freemasonry has a structure unlike that of almost any other Masonic organization in any jurisdiction. Freemasonry was introduced into Sweden by Count Axel Wrede-Sparre who had been living in Paris and was initiated into the Order there. In 1735 he gathered a group of friends, most of them members of the nobility, who had similar initiations and formed a Lodge. In 1752 'Lodge St Jean auxiliaire' was started in Stockholm, and shortly thereafter Freemasonry received Royal patronage, which it continues to enjoy to this day (see p. 304).

The Swedish Rite grew during the latter half of the 18th century, and today it confers eleven Degrees in three different Lodges: the Lodge of St John (I–III), the Lodge of St Andrew (IV–VI), and the Chapter (VII–X). The first three Degrees are not dissimilar to those practised in Craft Freemasonry, while the eleventh Degree is honorary and rarely awarded. The rituals include material from the 'British' Higher Degrees, the *Rite Ecossais*, and, according to some, mystical material from the work of Emanuel Swedenborg. The Swedish Rite is worked in Iceland, Finland, Norway (the sash left is Norwegian), Denmark and Northern Germany. It is unusual among Masonic Rites in that it admits only men of the Christian faith.

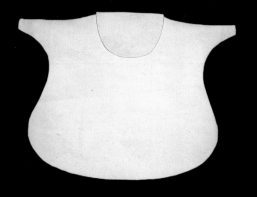
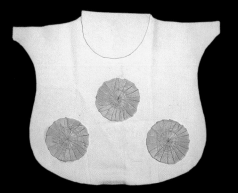
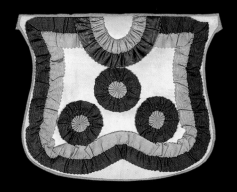

Top row (St John Degrees)
I Apprentice; II Fellow Craft; III Master Mason
Middle row (St Andrew's degrees)
IV–V Apprentice-Companion of St Andrew;
VI Master of St Andrew
Bottom row (Chapter Degrees)
VII Very Illustrious Brother, Knight of the East
VIII Most Illustrious Brother, Knight of the
West (these Degrees share an apron)
IX Enlightened Brother of St John's Lodge
Opposite (sash – there is no apron for this Degree)
X Very Enlightened Brother of St Andrew's
Lodge

5

Liberty, Equality, Fraternity

FREEMASONRY IN SOCIETY

*Since its formation Freemasonry has
been very active in society, most usually
through its charitable activities. The
illustration here, from c. 1802, is by
Brother Bartolozzi, Engraver to His
Majesty, and depicts a ceremony at the
Royal Masonic School for Girls.*

THE RELATIONSHIP between Freemasonry and wider society has always been mixed. On one hand the good works and significant charitable contributions have been widely applauded; on the other hand the Order's secrecy has been misunderstood, mistrusted and feared. Similarly, the large number of prominent Freemasons has led to a belief that the Order wields great political influence – for good and for bad – as well as to accusations of exclusivity, especially in relation to the non-admission of women.

At the time of its foundation the Masonic Order, it seems, was quite content to keep itself to itself – the sole aims of the Brethren meeting together in taverns or private homes were good fellowship and self-improvement, and there was no desire to proselytize, nor to engage with the outside world in any formal way. The meetings were closed, and most of the material discussed was kept secret. However, while it is important to note at the outset that Freemasonry was not established with the intention of being a direct influence in society, when the nobility and many prominent intellectuals started to join soon after its foundation the Order acquired an importance and philosophical influence disproportionate to its size. This sudden growth, combined with the practice of secrecy, inevitably roused public interest, and soon enough the Order was having to defend itself against any number of accusations.

As the Order became more and more organized it began to assert itself more confidently in public, through processions, cornerstone-laying ceremonies and impressive Grand Lodge buildings, and even through the display of Masonic symbols on everyday items. Especially in the late 19th and early 20th centuries, when arguably Freemasonry was at the peak of its popularity (along with other Fraternal or Friendly Societies such as the Oddfellows, which also acted as a positive social force), Masonic functions were important events in High Society, drawing great crowds.

This period also saw the foundation of many Masonic charities. In fact, the first Masonic charitable fund was established as early as 1727, by the premier Grand Lodge, for the care of 'poor and distressed Masons'. However, soon enough the charity extended beyond the fraternity to help the more vulnerable members of society through the construction and maintenance of hospitals, orphanages and schools. Charity remains every bit as important today for Freemasonry, and around the world millions of pounds are given to good causes, including Masonic homes, hospitals, medical research, and many other areas with benefits certainly not limited to Masons. Charity is one of the three Cardinal Virtues championed by Freemasonry, and it is worth remembering that the fundamental intent of the Order in every country has always been 'to make good men

The painting opposite presents the universal nature of Freemasonry, represented here as a woman to reflect the Order's charitable and humanitarian qualities. Beside her stand personifications of Silence and Truth, while all around are Masons of many cultures and faiths, identified by national or ethnic dress, including Scots, Chinese and Arabs.

better'. The qualities promoted by Freemasonry – honesty, truth, justice, equality, as well as charity – are qualities that every society needs, and all Masons are encouraged to take their responsibilities for practising Masonic teachings just as seriously outside the Lodge.

However, it cannot be denied that Freemasonry has also been perceived as exclusive, and it has received particular criticism over its non-admission of women. Why women were excluded from the original Order is difficult to say, though clearly the social role of women was very different in the 17th and 18th centuries. However, it is also worth noting that during that time there were many witch-scares, and witches were regularly burned. Since witches' covens are androgynous, it is not unreasonable to think that Freemasons, meeting in private and thought to be working with unknown things, would exclude women simply to ensure that they were not accused of witchcraft.

However, once Freemasonry had become known and attained a degree of respectability, provisions were soon made to involve women. The earliest of these were 'Adoptive Bodies', groups of men and women that met and participated in ritual Degrees analogous to, but not the same as, Masonic Degrees. These groups were 'adopted', and presided over, by Masonic Lodges. The first of these groups appeared in Paris in the mid-1700s, and the practice grew rapidly. The idea of adoptive bodies was very popular with the nobility, and by 1774 such groups were also to be found in the Netherlands and Germany. Adoptive Lodges continue today, but in the late 19th century mixed Lodges and exclusively female Lodges also began to form. Today there are all-female Lodges in Europe, Britain and the Americas. While not 'recognized' by all Masonic bodies, the United Grand Lodge of England provides Lodge facilities for Women's Grand Lodges, and works with them for mutual benefit.

Yet there remain detractors of Freemasonry, and the history of anti-Masonry is almost as old as that of the Order. The first serious anti-Masonic action, as we saw on p. 102, was by the Catholic Church, with the Papal Bull of 1738. However, this anti-Masonic sentiment soon spread to other parts of society, and even today deep suspicion is found in certain quarters. The general view underlying anti-Masonry seems to be that groups meeting in private and keeping secrets must be up to no good. When such groups are part of a prominent organization, they are perceived to be seriously dangerous. The motivation for anti-Masonic activity may be religious, personal or political; indeed, for a few years in the early 19th century there was even an Anti-Masonic Party in the United States.

But to return to the beginning, there is a part of Freemasonry that is very much about good fellowship and serious learning with the like-minded, regardless of background. In this sense Freemasonry is fundamentally egalitarian and inclusive.

The frame opposite contains many symbols of morality, to encourage an upright life. At the centre are the words Light, Life, Love, and Faith, Hope, Charity – the guiding principles of Freemasonry. The 19th-century French snuff box above is rich in Masonic symbols and emphasizes the qualities of Truth (left) and Justice (right).

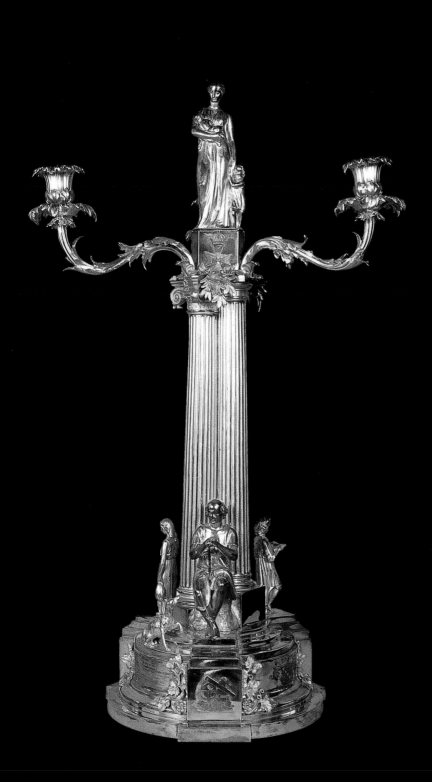

For Freemasons, Charity means many things. First, it is the highest of the Cardinal Virtues, as is illustrated in the 19th-century silver candelabra left, where 'Charity' is supported by Doric, Ionic and Corinthian Columns. Second, it is something to be practised among Brothers, as seen in the medal above, which is from the General Masonic Relief Association of the United States and Canada, formed in 1886 to provide assistance for Masons who were travelling away from their homes and families and, thus from their own Lodges. Finally, it is something to be practised in the context of wider society, as seen in the print opposite. In Europe the winter of 1789 was very severe, and French Freemasons undertook to provide relief for those suffering from the situation. The text round the edge of the image reads: 'Good Deeds unite the Citizens of the World from one Pole to the other'.

ROYAL FREEMASON'S SCHOOL FOR FEMALE CHILDREN,
ST JOHN'S HILL, BATTERSEA RISE.

The Cardinal Virtues of Faith, Hope and Charity appear often in Masonic art – opposite they are depicted on an engraved glass bowl, in the traditional Masonic Ladder between opposite verticals. From very early on Freemasons have worked to protect the welfare of those marginalized in society: the soup bowl above is from the Royal Masonic School for Girls, founded in 1788. A picture of the School buildings is shown in the centre of the bowl.

This photograph depicts the laying of the cornerstone of new buildings at Lord Mayor Treloar Hospital in Alton, England in 1929. Here we see the Pro Grand Master of the United Grand Lodge of England, Lord Ampthill, processing behind the Grand Sword Bearer (the same sword is illustrated on p. 108). Part of every ceremony of Cornerstone Laying includes the scattering of 'the corn of nourishment, the wine of refreshment and the oil of joy'.

Freemasons have long been associated with hospitals and medical charities. In 1922 the Ancient Arabic Order of Nobles of the Mystic Shrine (called Shriners) founded their first hospital to care for children with orthopedic problems. Today, in Canada, the United States and Mexico, twenty-two Shrine Hospitals provide orthopedic, burn and spinal-cord injury care as a charity to children under the age of eighteen.

While Freemasonry has always been essentially male, it is interesting to note that even in the earliest years women were involved in organizations close to the Order. After the Papal prohibition of Freemasonry in 1738, some Catholic Masons formed the Order of Mopses at Vienna. It was an androgynous Order, meaning that it admitted both sexes, while its name is derived from the German word *Mops*, meaning 'pug-dog'. The ceremony, above, depicts the reception of a lady into the Order.

The first genuine woman Freemason, however, was Elizabeth Aldworth (1693–1773), opposite, from Cork in Ireland. Her father, Viscount Doneraile, was a Mason and conducted Lodge meetings in his home, as was common practice early on (the events are said to have taken place shortly before the creation of the premier Grand Lodge in 1717). It is said that she was found to have observed a Masonic Degree by eavesdropping. The Brethren of the Lodge discussed the subject, and decided to confer the Degrees of the Order upon her in order to obligate her to secrecy. It is also said that in due course she became Master of that Lodge. Here she is shown in her Masonic regalia.

Here a lady is being received into a Lodge of Adoption. Adoptive Lodges were androgynous and operated under the direction of a regular Lodge. The Degrees they conferred were not the Masonic Degrees, but they had a distinctly Masonic flavour. Adoptive Masonry was very popular in continental Europe, particularly in France from the mid-18th century; and after the French Revolution the practice was revived in the spirit of egalitarianism. This watercolour depicts a ceremony conducted in France in the early 19th century.

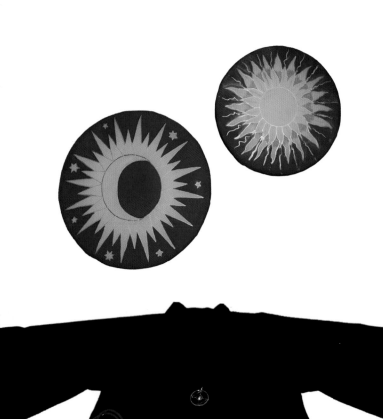

A more recent development has been the formation of exclusively female Lodges. These mirror the traditional male Lodges. The Women's Grand Lodge of Belgium, a participant in this movement it recent years has chartered three Women's Lodges in the United States.

In many respects the Women's Grand Lodge is more traditional than many 'traditional' Lodges. For example, when the Lodge is opened an Entered Apprentice draws the Masonic symbols with chalk on a blackboard on the floor of the Lodge. The Board is used during the Lodge's work, and it is erased when the Lodge is closed, just as happened in early Freemasonry. Similarly, the Women's Grand Lodge insists on specific regalia, shown to the right, consisting of a long black robe, the Lodge medal, and a very traditional apron (in stark contrast with many Lodges that allow rather casual dress). The Sun and the Moon, meanwhile, are displayed in the East of the Lodge. Lodge objects such as this are painted by members of the Lodge, again harking back to the very beginnings of Freemasonry in the early 18th century.

While traditional Freemasonry excludes women, the wives and sisters of Freemasons have always been encouraged to get involved in activities around the Lodge. The compact opposite must have belonged to the wife or sister of a Mason. The symbols are traditionally Masonic, but the background for the illustration is unusual; it is made of butterfly wings.

Nº 1314
ACACIA LODGE
WE SERVE

This photograph of English women Freemasons dates to the early 20th century, when female Masonry was in its infancy. The regalia is of the conventional English sort. The Master can be seen at centre, holding a gavel, emblem of her status, and wearing the sash of a 33° Mason in the Scottish Rite. Interestingly, most Women's Lodges have retained the nomenclature of traditional Freemasonry, and refer to each other as 'Brothers'.

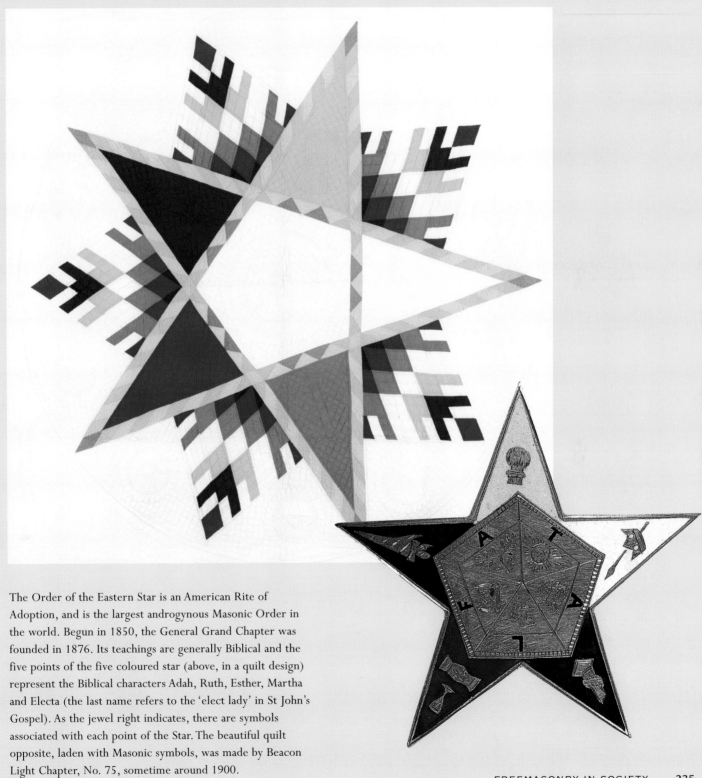

The Order of the Eastern Star is an American Rite of Adoption, and is the largest androgynous Masonic Order in the world. Begun in 1850, the General Grand Chapter was founded in 1876. Its teachings are generally Biblical and the five points of the five coloured star (above, in a quilt design) represent the Biblical characters Adah, Ruth, Esther, Martha and Electa (the last name refers to the 'elect lady' in St John's Gospel). As the jewel right indicates, there are symbols associated with each point of the Star. The beautiful quilt opposite, laden with Masonic symbols, was made by Beacon Light Chapter, No. 75, sometime around 1900.

Freemasons have always enjoyed good company, and not exclusively with Brethren. The ball shown opposite from 1883 commemorated the Prince and Princess of Wales, and was clearly a major event in society, reported in the press. The 19th-century bottle of liqueur above has the Square and Compasses cast into the glass, as well as the Royal Arch Triple Tau on the label. It may very well have been used at Festive Boards. On the other hand, some Grand Lodges prohibit the drinking of alcoholic beverages at Masonic functions.

It has always been fairly common for Masonic bodies to hold 'Festive Boards' after their meetings. These meals were and are often quite formal and certainly fraternal celebrations. The French Brethren opposite appear to be giving their attention to a Prayer of Thanksgiving prior to sitting down for dinner. It is clear that entertainment was to be provided here, although this was not, and is not, the case with all Festive Boards.

The song known as 'The Freemason's Health', right, first appeared in 1730. It celebrates the fraternal relationships enjoyed by the Brethren and assures them that the secrets of the Order will never be discovered by non-Masons. This song was popular well into the 19th century, and songs of this nature are still often sung at Festive Boards.

ANTIENT FREE AND ACCEPTED

MASONS OF ENGLAND.

GRAND FESTIVAL, FREEMASONS HALL,
WEDNESDAY 24TH APRIL, 1901.
H.R.H. The Duke of Connaught and Strathearn, K.G.
MOST WORSHIPFUL   GRAND MASTER.

GRAND STEWARDS 1901.

No. 99. SPENCER WILLIAM MORRIS, PRESIDENT.
No. 8. PERCY SLOPER,   No. 23. JOSEPH HUSBANDS,
          TREASURER.   SECRETARY.
No. 1. LT.-COL. EDWARD PRECE JONES M.P.   No. 26. COLONEL HY. TRAFFORD RAWLON,
„   2. FREDERICK E. BRISTOWE.   „ 29. JAMES R. EASTWOOD.
„   4. ROBERT LLEWELLYN DEVONSHIRE.   „ 46. CHARLES SPENCER PALMER.
„   5. COLONEL JOHN COPELL WRAY.   „ 58. HARRY RISCH MILLER.
„   6. HENRY W. HENDERSON.   „ 60. CAPTAIN WALTER FORD.
„ 14. ERNEST ALFRED WALKER.   „ 91. WILLIAM JAMES STYLES.
„ 21. RICHARD STAFFORD CHARLES.   „ 197. HARRY PASSMORE EDWARDS.
          No. 259. ROBERT PALGRAVE PAGE.

Grand Festivals are annual events, and the invitation to the
Festival of 1901 above indicates how open Freemasonry is
and how it is prepared to share much of the symbolism
which others claim it seeks to conceal. The Masonic calendar
contains many such events, commemorating the foundation
of Lodges, or important Saints' Feast Days. The punch bowl
opposite almost certainly would only be used on such very
special occasions. It was made for The Lodge of True
Friendship in Bengal, and the symbols on the side of the
bowl shown here relate to the Order of Knights Templar;
on the other side are the Craft symbols.

This punch bowl is possibly the largest Chinese export porcelain bowl in the world. It was made in 1813 for the Lodge of True Friendship, the first Lodge in Bengal, India. It holds nine-and-a-half gallons (about 43 litres) of punch. The recipe is as follows:

4 Quarts of 3 star brandy
4 Quarts good Jamaican Rum
4 Quarts Whisky
1 Quart Orange Curaçao
1 pint lime juice

2 tablespoons Angostura Bitters
2 sliced oranges
2 sliced lemons
Sliced skin of 1 cucumber
2 pounds of sugar

Garnish with a handful of fresh herbs and spices. Before drinking bottles of Bathgate soda were added by four Brethren standing around the bowl at North, East, South and West. The ration per member was one-fifth of a gallon (just under a litre).

The Antient Noble Order of the Gormagons was one of the earliest anti-Masonic organizations, with the first reference to the Order found in 1724, only seven years after the founding of the premier Grand Lodge. The engraving above by William Hogarth seems to parody a parade in which the Gormagons reveal the secrets of Freemasonry (Hogarth was himself a Freemason). In fact, the Gormagons never conducted any public parades, and all their activity was confined to newspaper articles critical of Freemasonry. These continued until 1731, after which the Order disappeared. No one is known to have been a Gormagon, but some speculate that the Order may have been a cover for the Duke of Wharton, the sixth Grand Master of the premier Grand Lodge who subsequently fell out with Freemasonry.

Critics have always tended to focus on the 'secrets' of Freemasonry. They suggest such things as the Mason's obligations of secrecy are intended to intimidate candidates, that secrecy would not be necessary unless Masons were up to no good, that secrecy conceals a private group that does business and makes deals unknown to the world. The print left shows a (probably apocryphal) episode in which a chambermaid, seeking to learn the Masonic secrets, climbed into an attic over the room and, while listening, slipped and fell thorough the ceiling. Upon hearing the commotion, inquisitive townspeople (including two clerics here) rushed into the Lodge hoping to find some evidence of iniquity.

ALL ON HOBBIES, GEE UP, GEE HO.!

The ubiquitous Apron, a fundamental part of Masonic regalia, appears to be parodied in the drawing of an 'Antimasonic Apron' opposite. However, the apron is actually anti-antimasonic, comparing the 'Hydra of Antimasonry' – breathing 'Infamy', 'Persecution' and 'Intolerance' – with Freemasonry, built on the Rock of Ages, and leading to perfection via the steps of 'Equal Rights', 'Honour' and 'Virtue'.

In 1826 in the United States, William Morgan, who claimed to be a Freemason, disappeared. It was alleged that he had been murdered by Freemasons for revealing Masonic secrets. In fact, no evidence of his death was ever discovered, but the idea was seized upon by anti-Masons and appeared widely in the press. Much anti-Masonic sentiment was generated, and an Anti-Masonic Party (seen in the cartoon above) was formed. The Party ceased to exist in 1836, but the negative impact of the affair on Freemasonry was huge.

Freemasonry has always been a rather easy target for satirists, with its ritual, dress and apparently arcane teachings – the 'Mummery of Masonry', as this cartoon has it. It was published in *Puck* magazine in its edition of 20 April, 1879. *Puck* was the first successful humour magazine in the United States, and it was noted for its satirical work on political and social issues (though it wasn't necessarily anti-Masonic). The overall tone of this cartoon is one of ridicule rather than opposition; several images relate to Masonic symbols and rituals, some of which do not exist, but which non-Masonic readers would have heard of in other anti-Masonic material. We can easily recognize references to the Square and Compasses, the Royal Arch Keystone, and the Death in the Third Degree – none of which is represented properly here.

THE MUMMERY

OF MASONRY— A RELIC OF THE DARK AGES.

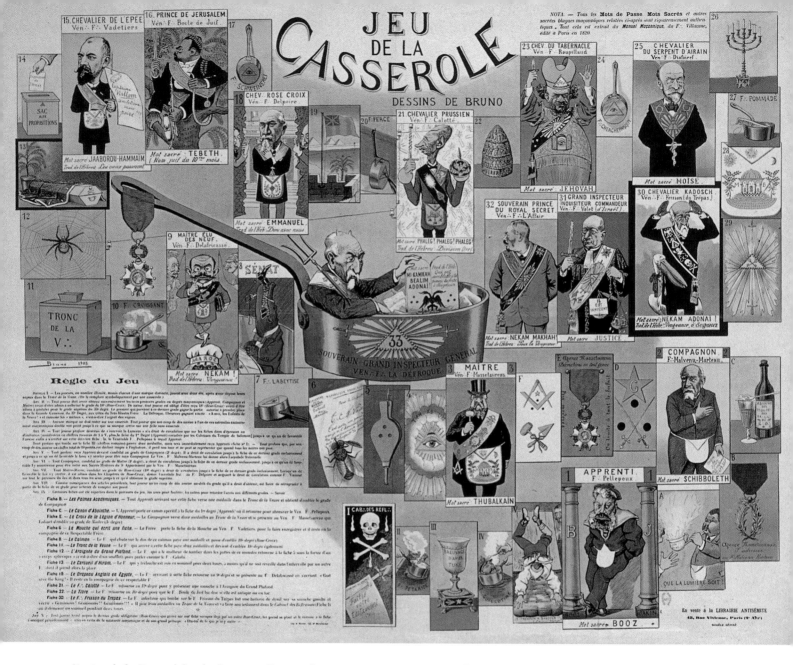

'Le Jeu de la Casserole' – the Saucepan Game – above, is an anti-Masonic board game, dating from 1905. In the centre of the board is a 33° Freemason sitting in a saucepan, while all around are symbols of other Degrees of the *Rite Ecossais*. This is not so much a board game to be played as a reference to Freemasonry as a game with a hidden purpose.

Among the various anti-masonic tracts published over the years, Léo Taxil's book, opposite, deserves special mention. Taxil was initiated in 1881, but never received further

Degrees, and was subsequently expelled. In 1885–6 he began his anti-Masonic activities, including books alleging to reveal all the secrets of the Order. The frontispiece of one of his books, opposite, implies violence as well as perpetuating the idea that Freemasons worship the Satan-like Baphomet (an accusation also levelled at the medieval Knights Templar). His books sold very well, but in 1897 he announced that all he had written in the past twelve years was a hoax. However, this has not stopped almost every exposé since from quoting him liberally.

LES MYSTÈRES
DE LA
FRANC-MAÇONNERIE

par

LÉO TAXIL

LETOUZEY & ANÉ, ÉDITEURS, 17, RUE DU VIEUX-COLOMBIER PARIS

— Buvons à l'extinction des vieux Fétichismes! ..

The cartoons above are from the French magazine *L'Assiette au Beurre* (The Plate of Butter). This satirical publication, somewhat like *Puck* (see pp. 246–7), was not specifically anti-Masonic, but again Freemasonry was a rather soft target. The masked man above clearly represents a 33° Mason, while the text at the bottom parodies the 'three dots' which are commonly used by French Masons to indicate abbreviations. In this case the abbreviation is of 'Les enfants de la veuve' – 'The Children of the Widow', a Masonic reference. The other cartoon, above right, shows another 33° Mason drinking a toast: 'Buvons a l'extinction des vieux Fétichismes!' – 'Let us drink to the extinction of old fetishes!'. The suggestion seems to be that even Freemasons are getting tired of the rituals of the Order.

The French poster opposite is altogether more sinister and disturbing. It was published by the Pétain regime during the Nazi occupation in 1941, and portrays the French valiantly struggling to build a new future, but being hindered by various aggressive groups, including the Gaulliste movement in England, the Jews, the Freemasons, and the 'Liars'; and it tells them to 'Leave us Alone!'. Freemasonry has generally been vilified and prohibited by totalitarian regimes, notably those of Mussolini, Hitler and Franco, all of which banned Lodges from meeting, destroyed and confiscated Masonic material and property, and particularly in Germany and Spain, sent Freemasons to their deaths. Franco even went so far as to write a book on the subject of Freemasonry, published under the pseudonym of 'J. Boor' – a reference to the columns 'Joachin' and 'Boaz'.

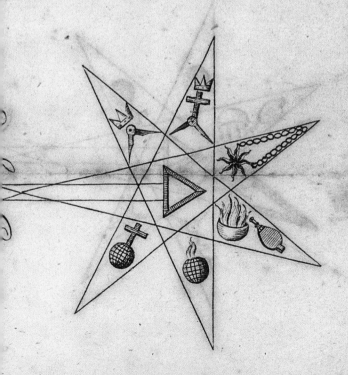

6

'Novus Ordo Seclorum'

MASONIC PUZZLES AND SECRETS

While to the outsider Freemasonry may well seem opaque, even within the Order there are sometimes factions that try to introduce new symbols and ideas – the drawing shown here is one such example by Brother William Finch. It is virtually impossible to interpret in a normal Masonic context, and remains something of an enigma even for Freemasons. Such modifications to the structure of Freemasonry are frowned upon.

MYSTERY has always surrounded Freemasonry, and understandably so. The arcane rituals, the guarded secrecy, and the accusations of power-mongering have all played their part in creating an aura of danger and otherworldliness. Here we look at the function of the secrecy, and some of the popular puzzles and myths that have grown up around the Order – the result, more often than not, of incomplete knowledge and active misinformation by those antagonistic towards Freemasonry.

We must begin with a fundamental truth: very few people who are not Masons understand Freemasonry as it really is. Since it is well known that Masons are obligated not to reveal certain things, many think of Freemasonry as a 'secret society', and for some the idea of a 'secret society' whose members are prominent in the social and business communities presents a real threat. Clearly, these conspiracy theorists reason, if influential people are involved in activities which must be kept secret, those people must be up to no good. From this frame of mind many conspiracy theories arise, and the nature of those theories depends on the political or philosophical orientation of the theorist. Freemasonry, as we have already seen, can be, and has been, attacked by all sides.

One of the most popular, and long-lasting, conspiracy theories is the idea that Freemasonry's objective is to establish a 'New World Order' – a worldwide government which controls every aspect of human life everywhere. This is an unattractive idea to almost anyone, and goes against one of the principal tenets of Freemasonry: liberty. Nonetheless, with some imagination the facts have been made to serve the paranoia. For example, the simple facts that George Washington was a Freemason and the first President of the United States 'prove' that the purpose

of the United States is to start such an order. Now a conspiracy industry has grown up around Washington, with any number of the Founding Fathers 'outed' as Masons, when clearly the majority were not. The fact that American citizens have always experienced the least governmental control of any population in the world is ignored.

In fact, specific conspiracy theories involving Freemasons are hard to come by. Two of the most prevalent stories – relating to the Dollar Bill (or, more correctly, the reverse of the Great Seal of the United States), which contains the 'All-Seeing Eye', and the planning of Washington, D.C. – are dissected here. The 'Masonic' All-Seeing Eye on the Dollar Bill has become something of a commonplace among conspiracy theorists, but it is worth running over the argument here. Washington is inconclusive to the point of insignificance.

Secrecy, itself, is another of the aspects of Freemasonry that causes some people concern. The Order categorically denies being a 'secret society'. Throughout this book there

The 'All-Seeing Eye' opposite is from an 18th-century Masonic Apron. The All-Seeing Eye is not a Masonic symbol, although it is a symbol frequently use by Freemasons to represent the Deity who observes all our motives and actions.

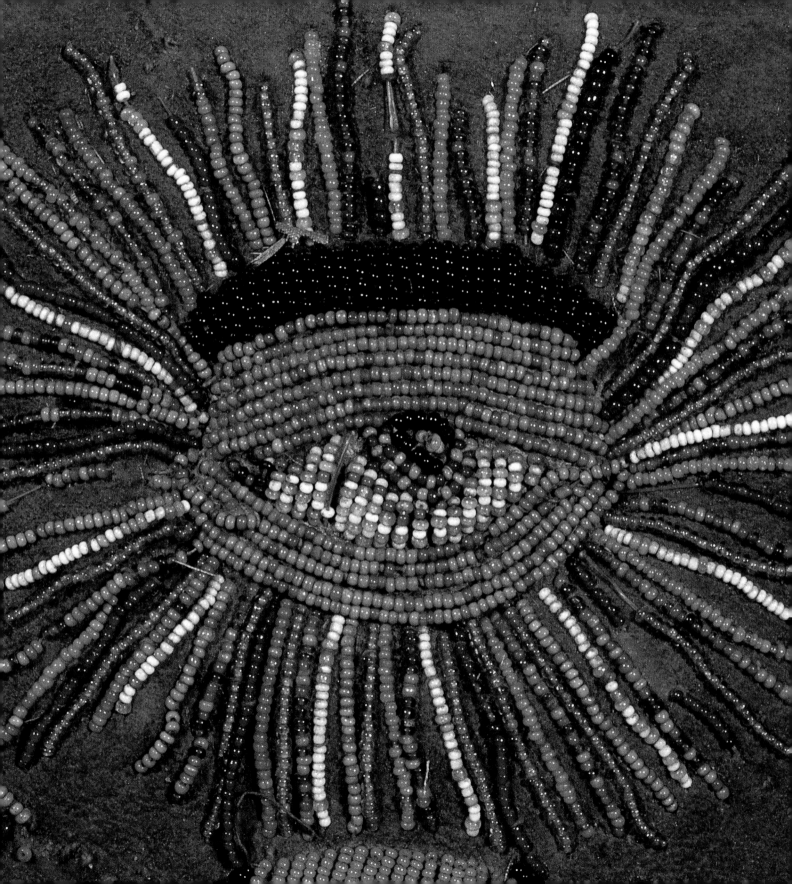

are several very prominent Masonic buildings; and if one walks down the streets of any sizable town one will find local Masonic buildings, less spectacular in their architecture, but all clearly identified as Masonic Halls. Is it possible that such an organization is a 'secret society'? 'Ah!', critics will say: 'Within the Order there is a small group of select members who pursue their conspiracies while keeping the others in ignorance'. As evidence of this they misrepresent quotations from prominent Masons who speak of the small group of Brethren who see the philosophical dimension of the Order, and use those quotations as evidence of the 'hidden group'. This is a difficult problem, since Freemasonry is forced to prove the absence of something – a contradiction of most Western legal systems.

Others still worry about the Masons' blood oaths, and supposed promises to always help Brothers, even, as some suggest, to the point of perjuring themselves. It is well known, through years of exposés, that there have been certain punishments associated with revealing secrets. However, the punishments were always intended to be figurative, and must be seen in the context of 18th-century societies, and the medieval stonemasons' guilds to which early Freemasonry looked when formulating its legislature. Recently some jurisdictions have dropped the threat of specific punishment as out of place in the 21st century, and, besides, there is no evidence of any such punishment having been carried out.

Another piece of evidence that is often cited to 'prove' that Masons have something to hide is their use of ciphers. In fact, Masonic ciphers, and everything that a Mason obligates himself to hold close, are available in any good library and certainly on anti-Masonic web sites. Freemasonry continues to practise this controversial idea because secrecy is a symbol that teaches a valuable principle: 'Do not tell things you know about yourself to those who cannot understand what you mean.' It is a principle that has been taught by respected teachers, especially spiritual teachers, throughout the ages.

And that brings us to another common misunderstanding about Freemasonry: isn't it a religion? The answer, in brief, is no. It has no sacraments, no dogma, and does not claim to offer salvation by any means. Its teaching of moral behaviour is not a means of achieving salvation by good works. This is discussed on pp. 272–7.

And so we have to conclude that the mystery that surrounds Freemasonry is in part a Masonic tool, and to an even larger part the product of misinformation and wild speculation.

The papier mâché box above has three symbols, not obviously Masonic at first glance, but, taken together, they depict the motto adopted by the United Grand Lodge of England: Audi, Vide, Tace *– See, Hear, be Silent. That motto relates to one of the symbols of Masonry that is most misunderstood, secrecy. The French plate opposite depicts a Candidate writing in a space representing the Chamber of Reflection. In a larger sense the scene reminds the Freemason of the scope and seriousness of his life and of the attention which he should give to the manner in which he lives it.*

And the Darkness Comprehendeth it not

No 7 S.T ANDREW STREET DUBLIN

Masonic Jewels, Medals, K.T. Stars, Lodge Candlesticks &c.&c. Also Jewellery work in the most correct & Elegant Stile

by Bro.rs James Brush &Son Masonic Jewellers to the G.L.d. Medals for Farming & other Societies done with Taste

J. Brush Sculp. Dublin. A.L. 5802.

J. Ford Sculp.

Businefs transacted for Ready Money only on the lowest Terms.

While not used prominently today, there exist a number of different calendars in Freemasonry – almost one for each major Masonic body. Each takes as its 'year zero' a different momentous event – for most Freemasons this is the creation of the World, 4,000 years before Christ (as calculated in the 18th century by an analysis of the Old Testament). This is the case with the Irish advertisement for Masonic supplies (including Craft, Holy Royal Arch and Templar regalia), left, which is dated 'A.L. 5802', meaning 1802. However, for other Orders the reference date relates to the rebuilding of Solomon's Temple. The example shown opposite, a North American Royal Arch certificate, is dated 'A.I. 2402' – 1872.

Craft Masons commence their era with the creation of the world, and use *Anno Lucis* (A.L.), 'in the year of light'. Add 4,000 years to the common era.

Scottish Rite Masons also commence their era with the beginning of the world, but using the Jewish chronology, *Anno Mundi* (A.M.) 'in the year of the world'. Add 3,760 to the common era. After September add an extra year.

Royal Arch Masons date from the year the second temple was commenced by Zerubbabel, *Anno Inventionis* (A.I.) 'in the year of the discovery'. Add 530 to the common era.

Royal and Select Masters date from the year in which the Temple of Solomon was completed, *Anno Depositionis* (A.Dep.) 'in the year of the deposit'. Add 1,000 to the common era.

Knights Templar commence their era with the organization of their Order, *Anno Ordinis* (A.O.) 'in the year of the Order'. Take 1,118 from the common era.

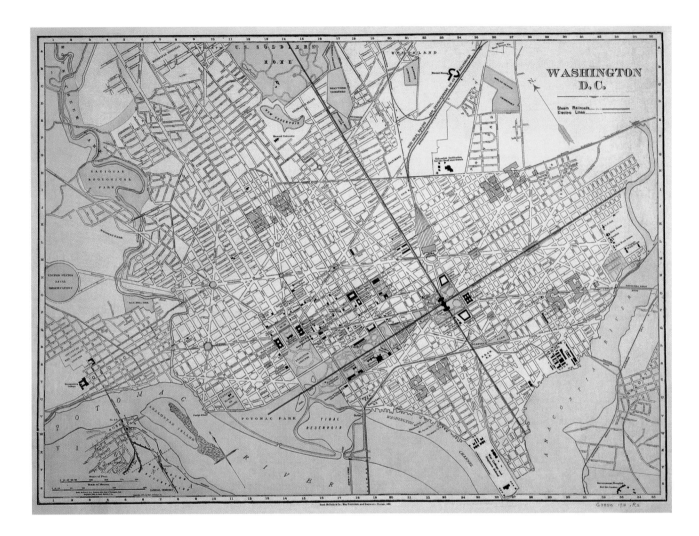

For many years a popular conspiracy theory has been that Washington, D.C. was founded on Masonic principles. In part this stems from the fact that Washington himself was a Mason, and wore his regalia when laying the cornerstone of the National Capitol Building of the United States, as shown opposite. Masonic cornerstone-laying ceremonies were very common in the early years of American history, and many anti-Masons have expressed concern that there was a Masonic conspiracy underlying the founding of the United States.

An embellishment of this theory is the idea that one can see Masonic figures – some thought to be sinister – in the layout of the city. A typical idea of this sort is the 'Square and Compasses' said to be centred on the Capitol Building, shown on the map

above. The layout of the city was the responsibility of Pierre l'Enfant, a French architect and engineer who was commissioned by George Washington, and it has been alleged that l'Enfant was a Freemason. Allegations of this sort are filled with fantasy, imagination and errors. There is no evidence that l'Enfant was a Freemason, and there were many others, also not Masons, involved in the planning of the Capitol. As the diagram above indicates, it is possible to find the Compass, but not the corresponding Square: Washington and Louisiana Avenues, that would form the Square, do not intersect but stop on either side of the Mall. The truth (disappointing for some) is that the layout of Washington, D.C. is not Masonic. It is based on geometric principles applied to the local topography.

Conspiracy theorists frequently point to the design of the US Dollar Bill – specifically the reverse of the Great Seal, as depicted on the Dollar Bill – as evidence of Masonic influence at the very highest positions in government. In particular, they point to the All-Seeing Eye – which they say is a Masonic symbol – and to the legend underneath, 'Novus Ordo Seclorum', which is frequently translated as 'New World Order'. Therefore, they conclude, the Freemasons are proclaiming that their desire is to create a New World Order.

This argument is flawed on both counts. First, the 'All-Seeing Eye', while used by Freemasons to remind themselves of the omnipresence of God (see left), is not a Masonic symbol; rather, it is a very old representation of the Deity. And neither is the pyramid a Masonic symbol. Since the design of the Great Seal dates to the late 18th century, the unfinished pyramid has thirteen levels – one for each state in the Union at that time. Seen in this context, the All-Seeing Eye is there to suggest that the people of America will depend on Divine guidance as they begin to develop their new Nation. 'Novus Ordo Seclorum', meanwhile, should actually be translated as the far more benign 'A New Order for the Ages' – a note of optimism to go with the start of the new nation and a representative government.

E PLURIBUS UNUM

The design of the Great Seal of the United States was by no means a quick and easy task. The work was accomplished by three separate committees which met between 1776 and 1782. The proposed design, opposite, was produced by Pierre Eugène du Simitière, a member of the First Committee. In the centre of the shield are emblems of the six nations from which the colonists came: Rose (England); Thistle (Scotland); Harp (Ireland); Fleur-de-lis (France); Lion (Holland); and Eagle (Germany). On the border of the shield are the initials of the thirteen States. The 'Eye of Providence' first appears not in the context of the pyramid, but rather above the shield. It is relevant to note that while some of the members of the committee were Freemasons, du Simitière was not.

The draft for the reverse side of the Seal (above) was produced by William Barton, an assistant to the Third Committee. Barton was twenty-eight years old and knowledgeable in the field of heraldry. He may very well have taken the idea of the 'All-Seeing Eye' from the design opposite, but incorporated it into his pyramid design, also picking up the number thirteen and building this into the levels of the pyramid. There is no record of Barton having been a Mason.

The final design of the Seal was created by Charles Thompson, for many years the Secretary of the Continental Congress and definitely not a Freemason. He gathered material from the work of the three Committees and submitted his design to Congress on 20 June, 1782.

MASONIC CRYPTOGRAPHY

While it is true that Masons do use ciphers on occasion, it is more for the sake of observing an obligation than for keeping a secret. This beautiful Italian sketch, in addition to several familiar Masonic emblems and symbols in the centre (many of which seem to relate to the Scottish Rite) contains a circular key to a cipher, showing each letter and its code equivalent. Set out again in triangular form upper right, it is a simple substitution cipher, a cryptographic device that was developed by Giambattista della Porta in 1563. Such ciphers are easy to crack so long as one is familiar with the language involved. In English, the most frequently used letters are contained in the word 'notaries'; and of those, 'e' is most common, then 't', then 'a', and so forth. To crack the cipher one need only see how frequently each character appears in a large text.

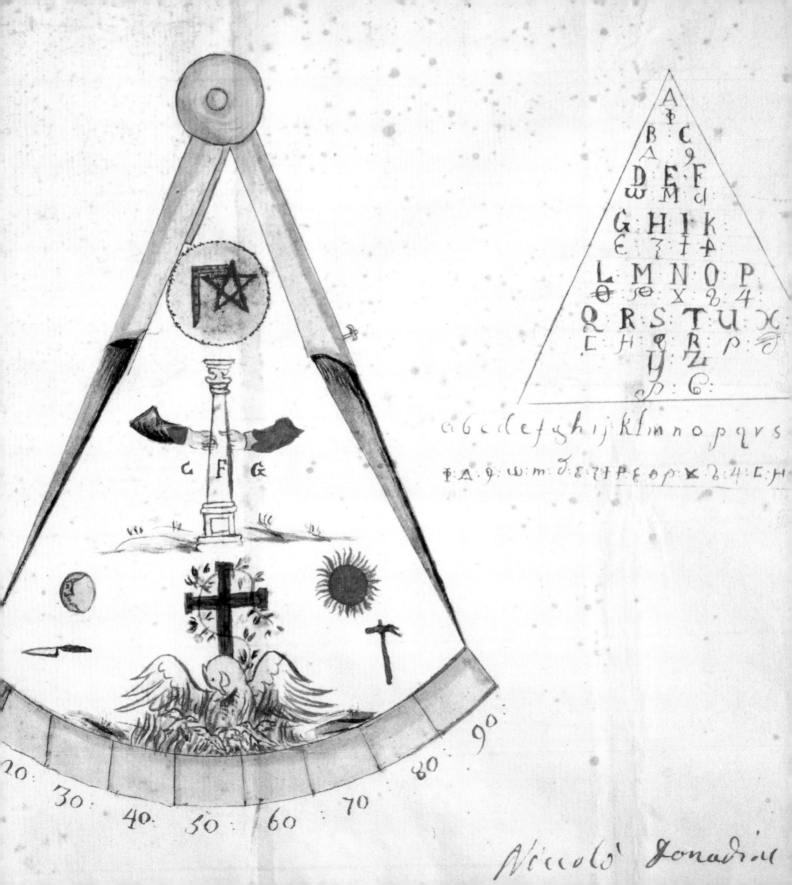

† PHILOSOPHIQUE.

Freemasons have always been interested in interrelationships between systems, and are fond of producing rather complex diagrams such as the one above, titled 'The Philosophical Cross'. At the centre of the Cross is the 'All-Seeing Eye', while around are the letters 'INRI' (*Iesvs Nazarenvs Rex Ivdaeorvm*). Cosmic references, including the Four Seasons and Four Ages of Man, are ample. The diagram seems to present material relating to the Royal Order of Scotland (the word *Ecosse* appears in abbreviated form as 'Ec:.'). The Royal Order

and the 'Rosy Cross', and appears to have flourished in France *c.* 1735–40 among Scottish Jacobite refugees. Prince Charles Edward Stuart granted a Charter to a Masonic Lodge in Arras in 1747, and on that document he described himself as Sovereign Grand Master of the Order of 'Rose Croix de Herodim de Kilwinning' – apparently referred to at the bottom right of the picture, in 'R:. C:. d'H:. c:. d:. m:. et de Kilwining'. The musical notes indicate the pattern of knocks associated with each Degree. This diagram seems to have been

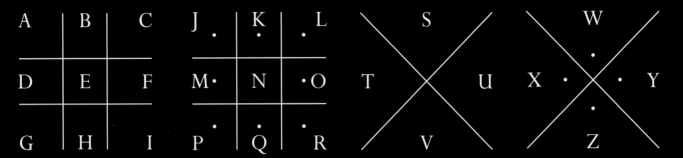

Key to cipher reading from left to right

Key to cipher reading from right to left

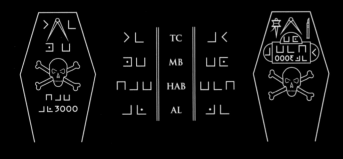

The cipher shown above is the 'Pigpen Cipher', sometimes called the 'Freemasons' Cipher'. It is said to have been invented by Masons in the early 18th century to facilitate correspondence while observing the commitment not to reveal certain things. Like other ciphers we have seen, this is a simple substitution cipher, and it is not a really useful way to keep valuable secrets. On the other hand, material for Masonic instruction can be printed by the use of such ciphers, as seen on the coffin of the Third Degree, left. 'AL', as we have already seen on p. 258, stands for *Anno Lucis*.

GRUNDLINIEN
EINES
EIFRIG ARBEITENDEN
FREIMAURER.
IN
DREIMAL
DREI.

LIEBE GOTT ÜBER ALLES UND DEINEN NÄCHSTEN WIE DICH SELBST

The use of ciphers seems to have been more common in the 18th century than it is today, perhaps because in those days substitution ciphers were less well understood and thus more difficult for non-Masons to crack. Certainly it would have been more difficult in a period when spelling was not standardized. The 18th-century Viennese manuscript opposite has part of the text at the bottom encrypted (though the reader will need to speak German to make sense of it).

The drawings right show the four faces and the top of a square stone with a pyramidal top. This cube is encountered in the ritual of the 14th Degree in the Scottish Rite (as practised by the Grand Orient of France and other continental Lodges), where it is discovered in a Secret Vault. There is a great deal of symbolic material here including some familiar Masonic symbols and a simple substitution cipher of the sort we have seen before.

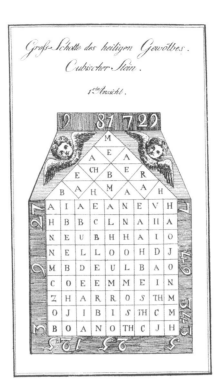

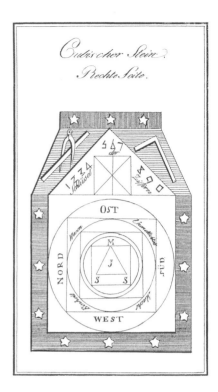

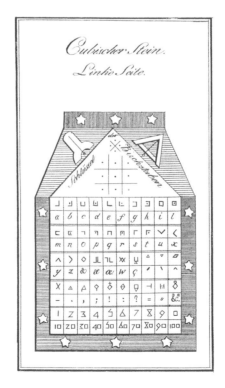

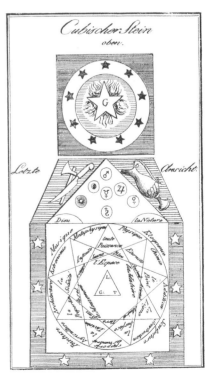

Many critics of Freemasonry have long maintained that the Order is a religion. In fact, although Freemasonry is by tradition a society of religious men, it is categorically not a religion. It has no theology; it offers no sacraments; and it does not claim to ensure, or offer a way to achieve, salvation after death. While its teachings can be interpreted to have a spiritual frame of reference, each Brother is expected to practise those teachings in the context of his own religion.

However, it must admitted that some Masonic activities may appear to be 'religious'. The picture above, for example, depicts what is sometimes referred to as a 'Masonic Wedding Ceremony'. This is not quite true. Certainly some jurisdictions, usually in Continental Europe, conduct Masonic ceremonies that 'reaffirm' marriage. However, the Master of a Masonic Lodge is not an agent legally authorized to perform a marriage, and so a couple who participate in a Masonic ceremony of this nature must already be married. Therefore it is solely an event for a married couple who want to celebrate their union with a group of personal friends. Part of the ceremony, depicted here, involves the pouring of water and wine into the same cup, to symbolize the couple's union.

The apron opposite is the sort worn at a 'Lodge of Sorrows', which is held at the request of the family or friends and Brethren of a deceased Brother as a memorial to his good life and service. Again, it is not a sacrament, nor does it replace any religious funeral service of a Brother's religion. It is simply a formal remembrance. Neither of these events are held in an open Lodge.

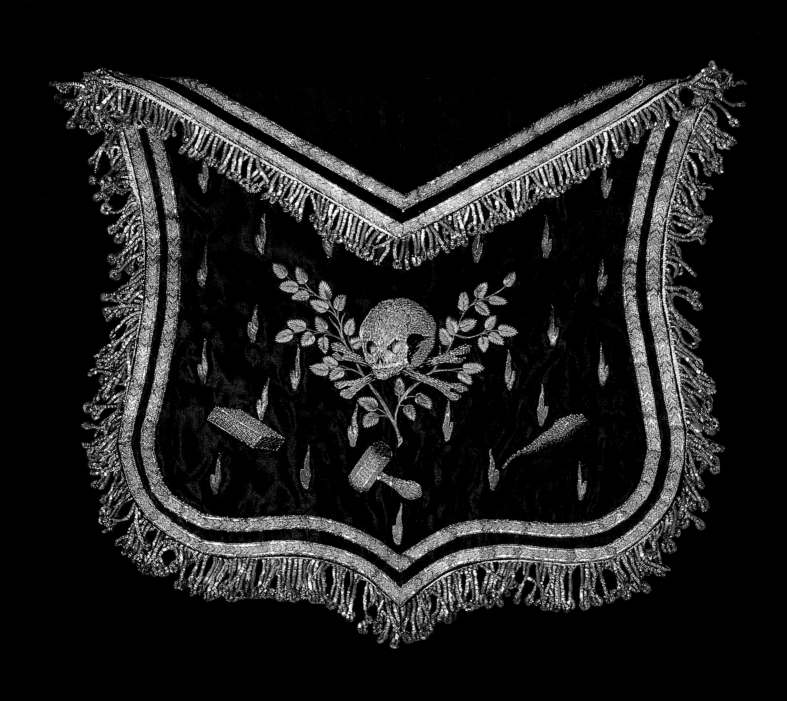

The House of the Temple in Washington, D.C., above, is the headquarters of the Scottish Rite, Southern Jurisdiction. Its structure is in large part modelled on the Mausoleum at Halikarnassos (*c.* 352 BC), one of the Wonders of the Ancient World. The architecture inspires the viewer and gives a glimpse of the foundations of Western Civilization. But why do Masons call such a place a 'Temple' – does this mean that it is a place of worship? Not necessarily. The original meaning of the word is a space set aside for a special purpose, and that need not be religious. In fact, the building's main purpose is ceremonial and administrative.

Under the Holy Royal Arch, opposite, is a pedestal illuminated by Divine Light. The pedestal is not, as some think, a place where Masons worship. It is a place that must be present in each of us. The letters refer to the builders of Solomon's Temple: Solomon, Hiram of Tyre, and Hiram Abiff.

The images opposite and above show the Three Great Lights in Masonry: the Volume of Sacred Law, the Square, and the Compasses. The Sacred Writings are open whenever a Lodge is working, and are used in taking obligations. However, the Candidate will be obligated on the volume that he considers to be sacred. And if there are Brethren of many faiths in the Lodge, then copies of Books sacred to each will be opened. The Square and Compasses can be understood in two ways.

First, they teach the Brother to square his actions by the Square of virtue while using the Compasses to circumscribe his desires and keep his passions within due bounds, the definition of virtue and the radius for circumscription being found in the Sacred Writings. Second, from the metaphysical point of view, the Sacred Writings can be understood to represent the Divine Source from which the Spirit (Compasses) and Soul (Square) emanate.

7

Brothers in Craft

PROMINENT FREEMASONS

*Throughout its history Freemasonry
has been privileged to include among
its Brethren Royalty, prominent
politicians, entertainers, scientists and
military personnel. In this illustration
from c. 1740, King Frederick II of Prussia
is conducting the adoption of Margrave
Friedrich of Brandenburg-Bayreuth
into Freemasonry.*

CARL·AUGUST·BEI·GOETHE.

T HOUGH FREEMASONRY is open to people from all walks of life, it has always had a good number of achievers in various fields. Particularly interesting is the way in which it has attracted people from very diverse backgrounds — from princes to jazz musicians, avant-garde artists to groundbreaking scientists, philosophers to astronauts…

The remarkable diversity of backgrounds found in Freemasonry has existed since the foundation of the Order in the early 18th century. Here we take note of some of the more prominent members of the Order over the last three centuries, and consider what might have attracted them to Freemasonry. In the Introduction we considered the wide-ranging interests of the two earliest known Freemasons, Robert Moray and Elias Ashmole (see p. 22). Both were founder members of the Royal Society, the oldest scientific society in the world, so this gives us an immediate background to the Order. Of course, science was very different in the 17th century, and was far less dismissive of the 'esoteric' and 'mystical'. Clearly there were other Freemasons in the 17th century, but due to the lack of records, we are forced to speculate. Another member of the Royal Society, Sir Isaac Newton, is a possible candidate – certainly many of his friends were Masons, and his interests covered everything from Egyptian hieroglyphs to alchemy. According to William Preston, Sir Christopher Wren, the architect of St Paul's Cathedral in London, became a Mason in 1691. Just seven years after the completion of this impressive monument in 1710, the premier Grand Lodge was founded in its shadow, and the building appears in various Grand Lodge documents (see pp. 64 and 106).

Opposite, the German Enlightenment philosopher and Freemason Johann Wolfgang von Goethe is visited by Duke Carl August in 1828.

From 1717 the picture of membership becomes clearer, though we are still forced to speculate, and even in the 20th century we cannot always be certain of a person's membership. The latter part of the 18th century is commonly known as the Enlightenment, and it is significant that many of the figures associated with this movement, including the German philosopher Goethe and the French writer Voltaire, were Freemasons. Through men such as Benjamin Franklin, who was the United States' commissioner in France from 1776 onwards, the ideals of the Enlightenment spread to North America, where they informed the Declaration of Independence – 'all men are created equal'. Many Freemasons of this period, such as Franklin, were at the vanguard of the abolitionist movement. The American War of Independence was followed by the Revolution in France, and again many of the French Revolutionaries were Freemasons, inspired by the American model to create a more just and egalitarian society.

Freemasonry has been particularly attractive to those practising in the fields of art and architecture, not surprisingly considering that much of the ritual relates to the design and building of Solomon's Temple, and that the Order traces its roots to operative masonry. Moreover, up to the 19th century architects still worked largely in the Classical idiom, using the Five Orders developed in the Renaissance (see p. 65). Therefore, it is entirely understandable that they would have found Masonic symbolism attractive. 18th-century architects who are known to have been Freemasons include Sir John Soane and Claude Nicholas Ledoux, while 18th-

century painters include the great satirist William Hogarth, perhaps best known for his morality cycle, *The Rake's Progress*.

The 19th century saw an explosion in membership, with Freemasons on every side of the political spectrum: revolutionaries and conservatives, kings and republicans. The century began in Europe with the Napoleonic Wars. Napoleon himself was not a Freemason, though many around him were, and he revived the Grand Orient. But even taking into account the differing interpretations around the world, what organization could claim members of such diverse characters as Marat, Winston Churchill, Garibaldi and Simón Bolívar? But this is not surprising, since Freemasonry does not pursue a particular political agenda – rather it teaches its members to trust their conscience and to obey the laws of the country in which they reside. Perhaps the one generalization that we can allow ourselves is that Freemasons have fought for liberty, and against oppression (both architect and sculptor of the Statue of Liberty were Freemasons.) Another adherent of Freemasonry was Joseph Smith, Jr, of the Church of Jesus Christ and the Latter Day Saints. He was made a Freemason in 1842, and certain Masonic teachings resurface in Mormon doctrine. Meanwhile human progress was greatly advanced by two other prominent Masons, James Watt, the inventor of steam power, and Edward Jenner, who first used vaccinations to rid the world of the blight of smallpox.

In the 20th century Freemasonry continued to attract some of the biggest names. In Hollywood, men such as Cecil B. DeMille, Douglas Fairbanks and Clark Gable, as well as entertainers such as Harry Houdini and a number of jazz musicians including Al Jolson, were all members, though active to differing degrees. Actors have always been drawn to Freemasonry, perhaps because of the theatrical nature of the rituals. (A jewel for an actors' Lodge, complete with Yorick's skull, a Shakespearean reference, appears on p. 10.) Similarly, Freemasonry has been popular in the military services since the very beginning, and it continued to attract men such as Lord Kitchener and US General Douglas MacArthur. Other well-known personalities included the explorer Captain Scott, and, later, Buzz Aldrin, the second man to walk on the moon, as well as Alexander Fleming, the discoverer of penicillin.

And who is a Freemason today? As ever, Freemasons are drawn from all walks of life. In the 18th century many were attracted to the philosophical side of the organization, and this remains an attraction today. Similarly, Masons have always enjoyed the sense of fellowship and support that they draw from their Lodge. For a long time in the 20th century it seemed that the social side of Freemasonry was emphasized over the philosophical side, but this seems to be changing again, and increasingly, men – and women – are drawn by the possibility of learning more about themselves and their place in the Universe while contributing to society.

The English architect Sir John Soane is shown opposite in his regalia of Grand Superintendent of Works, in which capacity he designed a new Grand Lodge Hall (p. 289) in the early 19th century. The jewel above is for a Chapter named after William Hogarth, a famous artist of the 18th century and Grand Steward.

Considering Freemasonry's supposed origins in building, and its architectural symbolism, it is not surprising that many architects over the years have been attracted to the Fraternity. Of these, Claude Nicholas Ledoux was one of the more mystically inclined, given to creating fantasies (such as the one opposite from 1804) which combine Ancient Egyptian and Classical forms. Ledoux was a member of the Royal Academy in France in 1773 and his work included Masonic symbols. He is thought to have been a Freemason, but sadly, records of that period are incomplete. The French painter Jacques-Louis David was a near contemporary of Ledoux, and was a fellow member of the Royal Academy, as well as an enthusiastic supporter of the French Revolution, and was elected to the Convention in 1792. It is often said that he was a Freemason – many of that time in France were – and works such as the much-admired *Oath of the Horatii*, which some have read as an allusion to the oath that a Freemason takes, have been used as proof of this by historians.

Artists have continued to be attracted to Freemasonry. Some perhaps unexpected names include Marc Chagall, seen opposite just two years after his initiation in Russia in 1912, and the Spanish Cubist painter and sculptor Juan Gris, who was initiated with the artist Jacques Lipchitz into the Voltaire Lodge in Paris. The work above, *The Three Masks*, dates to the year of Gris's initiation, 1923. Other artists have been even more involved in Freemasonry: the Czech Art Nouveau artist Alphonse Mucha, for example, was the first Sovereign Grand Commander of the Supreme Council Ancient and Accepted Scottish Rite in his home country in 1923. It is widely thought the well-known Danish sculptor Bertel Thorvaldsen was a Freemason, and the fact that there is a Lodge named after him is suggestive.

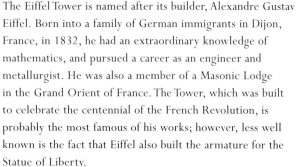

The Eiffel Tower is named after its builder, Alexandre Gustav Eiffel. Born into a family of German immigrants in Dijon, France, in 1832, he had an extraordinary knowledge of mathematics, and pursued a career as an engineer and metallurgist. He was also a member of a Masonic Lodge in the Grand Orient of France. The Tower, which was built to celebrate the centennial of the French Revolution, is probably the most famous of his works; however, less well known is the fact that Eiffel also built the armature for the Statue of Liberty.

The design of the Statue, meanwhile, was the creation of another French Freemason, Frédéric Bartholdi. Presented in 1894 as a gift to the American People from the People of France the work was designed to act as a symbol of the values which the two countries shared (and which Freemasons hold dear). Brother Bartholdi was one of the first members of Lodge Alsace-Lorraine in Paris, which was largely composed of writers, artists and intellectuals.

Early Freemasons met in taverns, but in 1776 the English Grand Lodge built Freemasons' Hall in Great Queen Street to provide Lodge Rooms. In the early 19th century Freemasons' Hall was modified and extended by the renowned architect Sir John Soane (see p. 282), who was the first Grand Superintendent of Works. The Lodge Room in the New Hall, opposite, is one of his creations.

Many writers have been drawn to Freemasonry. Rudyard Kipling, opposite, famous author and poet of the British Empire, whose works include *The Jungle Book*, was initiated in Lodge of Hope and Perseverance No. 728 in 1882. Much of his writing, and particularly his poetry, describes experience of the Royal Army while making frequent Masonic references. The remarkable author and playwright Oscar Wilde, above, was born in Dublin in 1854. He attended Oxford University and was initiated in Apollo University Lodge No. 357. Jonathan Swift, above left, was also born in Dublin, in 1667. He entered the clergy and became Dean of St Patrick's Cathedral in 1713. He wrote *Gulliver's Travels* and other social commentaries, and was also known for his remarkable charitable contributions. He is believed to have been a member of Lodge Goat-at-the-Foot-of-the-Haymarket No. 16 in London. Born in 1694, Voltaire (whose real name was François-Marie Arouet) was a satirical writer and critic of the French aristocracy for which he spent some time in the Bastille. In the 1740s he was a diplomat for Louis XV and was elected to the French Academy in 1746. He was initiated in Loge des Neuf Soeurs, Paris, in 1778, only a few months before his death.

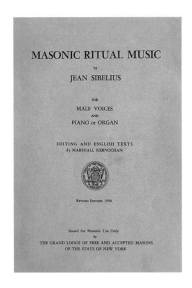

MASONIC RITUAL MUSIC
by
JEAN SIBELIUS

FOR
MALE VOICES
AND
PIANO or ORGAN

EDITING AND ENGLISH TEXTS
by MARSHALL KERNOCHAN

REVISED EDITION, 1950

Issued for Masonic Use Only
by
THE GRAND LODGE OF FREE AND ACCEPTED MASONS
OF THE STATE OF NEW YORK

Perhaps the best-known musician Freemason is Wolfgang Amadeus Mozart, who has had many Lodges named after him (see the jewel, left), and who appears in the painting on pp. 88–9. He was initiated in Charity Lodge in 1784; a year later his friend Franz Haydn (top left) was initiated into the same Lodge. His most 'Masonic' work is The Magic Flute; the stage set opposite was designed by Karl Schinkel, and captures a spirit of ancient intrigue and mystery. There is no positive evidence that Ludwig van Beethoven (top right) was a Mason, but many of his acquaintances were (he met Mozart in 1787) and his works and correspondence contain many apparently Masonic references.

And Freemasonry has continued to attract musicians more recently. The Finnish composer Jean Sibelius, for example, was initiated in Suomi Lodge No. 1 in 1922, and composed various selections for use in the Masonic Lodge workings (top left). And even more recently both George Gershwin (bottom left) and Jazz musician Louis Armstrong (bottom right) claimed to be Freemasons, though the details of their memberships are not clear.

Laurel and Hardy formed one of the best-known comedy teams of the early 20th century. Stanley Laurel was born in England and emigrated to the United States as a Vaudeville actor in 1910. Oliver Hardy was born in Georgia, United States, and was initiated into Masonry in Solomon Lodge, No. 20, in Jacksonville, Florida. They are shown opposite in the 1933 comic film *Sons of the Desert*, a parody of the Masonic Order of the Mystic Shrine.

David Garrick, above, was one of the foremost Shakespearian actors of his time. His career started with a performance of Richard III in 1742 and he continued to work as an actor and manager of Drury Lane Theatre until retiring in 1776. Garrick is thought to have been a Freemason; but as Lodges in the 18th century did not keep excellent records, there is no record of his membership. A snuff box in possession of St Paul's Lodge No. 194 suggests that Garrick had been a Mason. Here he is depicted between personifications of Tragedy and Comedy, painted by Sir Joshua Reynolds in 1760–61.

James Watt was born in Greenock, Scotland, in 1736. He started to investigate steam engines at the University of Glasgow in 1761, and the improvements he introduced had a remarkable effect in facilitating the growth of the Industrial Revolution. One of the most imaginative inventors of the 18th century, he spent his years of retirement, after 1800, working with optical devices. He was initiated into Freemasonry in 1763. Here he is depicted holding compasses, symbol both of his profession as a scientist and of his status as a Freemason.

Robert Falcon Scott, above, called 'Scott of the Antarctic', was born in Devonport, England in 1868 and was a Captain in the Royal Navy. Ernest Henry Shackleton was born in County Kildare, Ireland in 1874 and was a certified Master in the Merchant Marine. Scott was initiated in Drury Lane Lodge, No. 2127 in 1901; Shackleton was initiated in Navy Lodge, No. 2616 in 1901, and served as Scott's Third Lieutenant on the National Antarctic Expedition of 1901–4. Some biographers have suggested that there was great animosity between the two, but more recent research has indicated that they were good friends on the expedition. Scott subsequently joined Royal Navy Lodge, and died in 1912 on his failed attempt to reach the South Pole. Shackleton made three additional voyages of exploration to Antarctica, and was knighted for his efforts.

Edward Eugene 'Buzz' Aldrin was a fighter pilot in the U.S. Air Force, and a member of Clear Lake Lodge, No. 1417 in Seabrook, Texas. In 1963 he was selected to be a NASA Astronaut, and on 20 July, 1969, the Apollo 11 Lunar Mission landed; and 'Buzz' Aldrin, the pilot for the Mission, was the second human being to step onto the Moon. He took with him a flag of the Scottish Rite (opposite), hand-made by Ms. Inga Baum, then the Librarian at the House of the Temple in Washington, D.C. The flag was returned and is now on display at the House of the Temple.

SUPREME COUNCIL 33°

SOUTHERN JURISDICTION, U.S.A.

DEUS MEUMQUE JUS

King Edward VII, opposite, was initiated in 1868 in Stockholm by the King of Sweden, and became the Grand Master of the United Grand Lodge of England in 1875. He was an active Freemason and conducted Masonic ceremonies laying the cornerstones of buildings throughout the land. He was the Worshipful Master of several Lodges including Apollo University Lodge, No. 357 at Oxford, Royal Alpha Lodge, No. 16, and Prince of Wales Lodge, No. 259 in London. He was also an Honorary Member of Edinburgh Lodge, No. 1 in Scotland. According to the custom of Royal Grand Masters, upon ascending to the throne he resigned the position of Grand Master and assumed the title of 'Protector of the Craft'. His brother, the Duke of Connaught, was installed as Grand Master. The casket below, made of Indian silver and containing a Loyal Address, was presented to Edward while Prince of Wales in 1876 during his visit to Bengal.

King George VI, left, was initiated in Naval Lodge No. 2612 in 1919, and in 1922 he became the Senior Grand Warden of the United Grand Lodge of England. He ascended to the throne in 1936 and was installed as the Grand Master of Scotland in that year. He was the first English Monarch to participate in Masonic ceremonies. His feelings for Freemasonry are summarized in this quotation: 'The world today does require spiritual and moral regeneration. I have no doubt, after many years as a member of our Order, that Freemasonry can play a most important part in this vital need'.

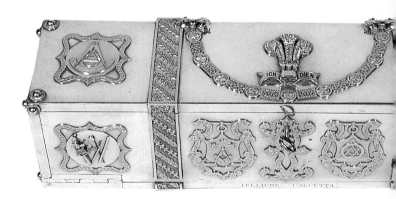

ROOSEVELT THE MASTER MASON

© 1912
J.L. PHELPS
SPOKANE

George Washington, Commander of the Colonial Army during the American Revolution and first President of the United States, was made a Mason in Fredericksburg Lodge, Virginia in 1752–3. He was Worshipful Master of Alexandria Washington Lodge, No. 22 in 1788–9, and his Masonic activities are revered at the George Washington Masonic National Memorial in Alexandria, Virginia.

Theodore Roosevelt, left, was born in New York City in 1858. Among many other activities he led the 'Rough Riders' Cavalry Regiment in the Spanish–American War, was Governor of New York, Assistant Secretary of the Navy, initiator of the Panama Canal, as well as a conservationist and a rancher in North Dakota. He was Vice President when President William McKinley was assassinated; and, at 42, he became the twenty-sixth President of the United States. He was the youngest person to hold the office which he occupied from 1901 to 1909. He was made a Mason in Matinecock Lodge, No. 806 in Oyster Bay, New York. He died in Oyster Bay in 1919.

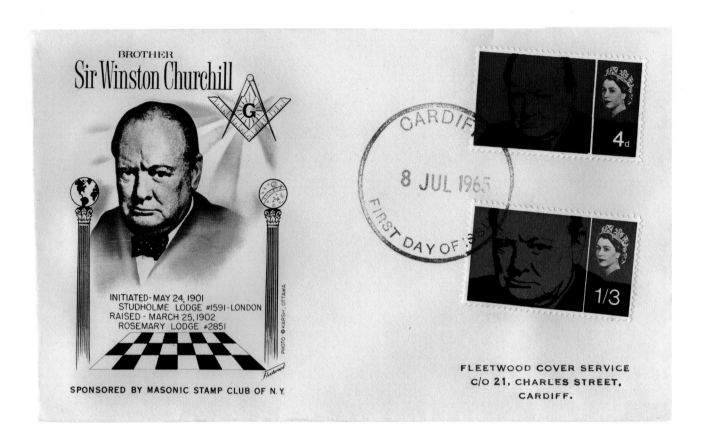

Winston Churchill was one of the most remarkable political leaders in the history of Western civilization. He was initiated into Freemasonry in Studholme Lodge in London in 1901, and he attended regularly until 1912; in 1918 he was among the petitioners for a Charter for 'Ministry of Munitions Lodge', but the Charter was not granted. During this period his political life was becoming very complex, and that may account for his minimal Masonic activity. Churchill was Prime Minister of Great Britain during the Second World War, and it is for his outstanding leadership in that context that he is most remembered and appreciated.

Britain is not the only country where the Royal family is involved in Freemasonry. In Sweden the Swedish Rite has been closely associated with the Royal family since the late 18th century. King Charles XIII, opposite, ascended to the throne in 1809, retaining the previously held position of Grand Master. He was so enthusiastic about Freemasonry that he created the 'Order of Charles XIII', open only to Freemasons.

In the 19th century Freemasonry attracted many who were striving against injustice and oppression. One such man was Giuseppe Garibaldi (opposite right below), who in 1844, at the age of 37, joined Lodge 'Les amis de la Patrie' in Montevideo. He was a Naval Officer for the navy of Piedmont and a leader of volunteer forces against the Austrians in Italy. He is greatly respected for his contribution to the formation of the Italian state. While he used Freemasonry as a political force – a goal which is contrary to the fundamental principles of the Order – he was also instrumental in the formation of the Rite of Memphis-Misraim. Another important force for change in the 19th century was Simón Bolívar (1783–1836), the South American liberator and founder of six modern-day states: Venezuela, Colombia, Panama, Ecuador, Peru and Bolivia. Initiated in Cádiz, Spain, he was involved with the Knights Templar and Scottish Rite and founded 'Order and Liberty' Lodge No. 2 in Peru.

ADDRESSES OF MASONIC ORGANIZATIONS

This is a list of contact details, including websites, for Grand Lodges and Masonic organizations around the world. Because of the large number of different Masonic jurisdictions, this is not exhaustive; however it does give a very good overview. 'F&AM' stands for 'Free & Accepted Masons' – 'AF&AM' stands for 'Ancient, Free and Accepted Masons'.

INTERNATIONAL BODIES

The International Order of Co-Freemasonry 'Le Droit Humain'
Le Droit Humain is open to men and women equally and has Federations and Lodges in seventy countries around the world, including Britain and the United States. It works the Ancient and Accepted Scottish Rite from the First to the 33rd Degree – thus providing initiatory continuity from the 'Craft' to the 'Higher' Degrees within the one Order. Several countries also work allied degrees of the York Rite in addition. Information on the Order worldwide can be obtained from the headquarters:

5, rue Jules Breton,
75013 Paris, France
www.droit-humain.org

ARGENTINA

Grand Lodge of Argentina
C/ Teniente General Perón 1242
Buenos Aires 1038
www.masoneria-argentina.org.ar

AUSTRALIA
There is a Grand Lodge for every state.

Grand Lodge of New South Wales
279 Castlereagh St, Sydney
www.uglnsw.freemasonry.org.au
Grand Lodge of Queensland
Box 2204, G.P.O., Brisbane,
Queensland 4001
www.uglq.org.au
Grand Lodge of S. Australia and N. Territory
PO Box 19, Rundle Mall, Adelaide
www.freemasonrysaust.org.au
Grand Lodge of Tasmania
3 Sandy Bay Road, Hobart, 7005
www.freemasonrytasmania.org
Grand Lodge of Victoria
300 Albert Street, East Melbourne,
Victoria 3002
www.freemasonsvic.net.au
Grand Lodge of Western Australia
P.O. Box 691, Victoria Park, WA 6979
www.gl-of-wa.org.au

AUSTRIA

Grand Lodge of Austria, AF&AM
Rauhensteingasse 3, A-1010 Vienna
Grand Orient
See website for contact details:
www.freimaurer.at

BELGIUM

Regular Grand Lodge of Belgium
rue Royale 265, B-1030
Brussels
www.glrb.org
Women's Grand Lodge of Belgium
BP no. 10050, B-1190 Brussels 19
www.mason.be/en/glf/index.htm
Grand Orient of Belgium
rue de Laeken, 79, B-1000 Brussels
www.gob.be
Grand Lodge of Belgium
See website for contact details:
www.glb.be

BENIN

Grand Lodge of Benin
03 BP 2106 Cotonou

BOLIVIA

Grand Lodge of Bolivia
See website for contact details:
www.geocities.com/Athens/7784/glb98.html

BRAZIL
There is a Grand Lodge for every state – they are all linked from the website of the Grand Orient, below.

Grand Orient of Brazil
AV.W-5 Quadra 913, Conjunto H,
Cep 70390-130, Brasília
www.gob.org.br
Grand Lodge of Brazil
SGAN 909, Módulo B, Asa Norte,
Cep 70790-090
www.guara.com.br/glmb

BULGARIA

United Grand Lodge of Bulgaria
See website for contact details:
www.grandlodge-bulgaria.org

BURKINA FASO

Grand Lodge of Burkina Faso
01 BP 3377 Ouagadougou 01

CANADA

Grand Lodge of Alberta
330-12 Ave. SW, Calgary T2R 0H2
www.freemasons.ab.ca
Grand Lodge of British Columbia &Yukon
1495 West 8th Ave., Vancouver
www.freemasonry.bcy.ca
Grand Lodge of Manitoba
420 Corydon Ave., Winnipeg R3L 0N8
www.grandlodge.mb.ca
Grand Lodge of New Brunswick
P. O. Box 6430 Sta. 'A',
Saint John E2L 4RS
www.glnb.ca
Grand Lodge of Newfoundland and Labrador
P.O. Box 23018, St John's A1B 4J9
www.newcomm.net/masonic/main.htm
Grand Lodge of Nova Scotia
1533 Barrington St,
Halifax B3J 1Z4
www.grandlodgens.org
Grand Lodge of Canada in Ontario
363 King St. W., Hamilton L8P 1B4
www.grandlodge.on.ca
Grand Lodge of Prince Edward Island
P.O. Box 337, Charlottetown
C1A 7K7
www.freemasonry.pe.ca
Grand Lodge of Quebec
2295 rue St Marc, Montreal H3H 2G9
www.glquebec.org
Grand Lodge of Saskatchewan
1930 Lorne St., Regina S4P 2M1
www.masons.sk.ca
National Grand Lodge of Canada
3940 Bergerac, Brossard Quèbec,
J4Z 2L6
www.glnc.org

CHILE

Grand Lodge of Chile, AF&AM
Marcoleta No. 659 Casilla 2867
www.granlogia.cl
Women's Grand Lodge
See website for contact details:
www.geocities.com/glfem

CHINA (TAIWAN)

Grand Lodge of F&AM
10, Lane 201, Chang-an East Road

COLOMBIA

National Grand Lodge
Carrera 49E No. 102-30
Barranquilla
Grand Lodge of Colombia
See website for contact details:
www.geocities.com/glcolombia

Western Grand Lodge
Carrera 4 No 13 – 24, Piso 17
Santiago de Cali
www.glodc.org.co
Serenisima National Grand Lodge
C/ San Juan de Dios Nro. 3-25,
Cartagena de Indias
www.serenisimagranlogia.com
Grand Lodge of the Andes
Carrera 25 No. 45-13 - B. Nuevo
Sotomayor, Bucaramanga
www.granlogandes.org
Eastern Grand Lodge
See website for contact details:
www.granlogiaoriental.org
Northern Grand Lodge
See website for contact details:
www.glnortecolombia.org

COSTA RICA

Grand Lodge of Costa Rica
Apartado 10060 – 1000 Avenida
Central, Calle 19 San José
www.granlogiacostarica.org

CROATIA

Grand Lodge of AF&AM
See website for contact details:
www.freemasonry-croatia.org

CUBA

Grand Lodge of Cuba
See website for contact details:
www.freemasonry.org/cuba

CZECH REPUBLIC

Grand Lodge of the Czech Republic
P.O. Box 99, CZ-111 21 Prague 1
www.freemasonry.cz
Grand Orient
See website for contact details:
www.zednari.cz

DENMARK

Danish Order of Freemasons
Blegdamsvej 23, Postbox 2563,
DK 2100 Copenhagn Ø
www.ddfo.dk

DOMINICAN REPUBLIC

National Grand Lodge
C/ Arzobispo Portes No. 554,
Esquina Las Carreas, Ciudad Nueva,
Santo Domingo

ENGLAND
Some of these organizations also have jurisdiction over Wales.

United Grand Lodge of England
Freemasons' Hall, 60 Great Queen St, London WC2B 5AZ
www.ugle.org.uk
The Order of Women Freemasons
27 Pembridge Gardens, London W2 4EF
Honourable Fraternity of Ancient Freemasons (Women only)
402 Finchley Road, Childs Hill, London NW2 2HR
www.hfaf.org
Supreme Grand Chapter of Royal Arch Masons of England
Address as for UGLE, above.
www.grandchapter.org.uk
Grand Lodge of Mark Masons
Mark Masons' Hall, 86 St James's St, London SW1A 1PL
Mark Masons' Hall also acts as a point of contact for various other Orders, including the Secret Monitor, the Knights Templar, the Royal Ark Mariners, etc.
Supreme Council Ancient and Accepted Scottish Rite
10 Duke Street, St James's, London
'The Operatives'
See website for contact details:
www.operatives.org.uk
Societas Rosicruciana in Anglia
Stanfield Hall, 88 Hampstead High St, London NW3 1RE
www.sria.uk.net

EQUADOR

Grand Lodge of AF&AM
Lorenzo de Garaycoa No. 821 y Avda. 9 de Octubre, 2do. piso, oficina No. 205
www.granlogia.org.ec

ESTONIA

Grand Lodge of Estonia
Postkast 3992, 10509 Tallinn
www.eestisl.ee

FINLAND

Grand Lodge of F&AM
Kasarmikatu 16 D, 00130 Helsinki
www.vapaamuurarit.fi

FRANCE

Grand Orient of France
16, rue Cadet, 75009 Paris
www.godf.org

Grand Lodge of France
8, rue de puteaux, 75017 Paris
www.gldf.org
Women's Grand Lodge of France
60, rue Vitruve, 75020 Paris
www.glff.org
National Grand Lodge of France
12, rue Christine de Pisan, 75017 Paris
www.grandelogenationalefrancaise.com
Grand Lodge of Master Mark Masons
See website for contact details:
www.glmmmf.org
Symbolic Grand Lodge of France
Fédération Constant Chevillon, 60 Bd de la Guyane, 94160 Saint-Mandé
www.grandelogesymboliquedefrance.org
Traditional and Symbolic Grand Lodge of the Opera
See website for contact details:
www.gltso.org

GABON

Grand Lodge of Gabon
BP. 233 Libreville, Gabon

GERMANY
In Germany four of the various Grand Lodges have together formed the United Grand Lodges of Germany.

United Grand Lodges of Germany
Emser Str. 10, 10719 Berlin Wilmersdorf
www.freimaurer.org
Women's Grand Lodge
Emser Str. 12/13, 10719 Berlin
www.freimaurerinnen.de
Grand Orient of Germany
Werdohler Landstraße 297, 58513 Lüdenscheid
www.sgovd.org

GREECE

Grand Lodge of Greece AF&AM
19 Acharnon St, Athens 10438
www.grandlodge.gr
National Grand Lodge of Greece
See website for contact details:
www.nglgreece.org

GUATEMALA

Grand Lodge of Guatemala
12 avenida 26-67 z. 05, Ap. Post. 01901, Guatemala City, CA
www.granlogiaguatemala.com

HONDURAS

Grand Lodge of AF&AM
Ap. Post. No. 20, La Ceiba, Atlantida

HUNGARY

Symbolic Grand Lodge of Hungary
Pf. 395, 1446 Budapest
www.szabadkomuves.hu
Grand Orient of Hungary
Pf. 595, 1398 Budapest,
www.nagyoriens.hu

ICELAND

Icelandic Order of Freemasons
P.O. Box 5151, Reykjavik
www.frmr.is

INDIA

Grand Lodge of AF&AM
Janpath, New Delhi 110001
www.masonindia.org

IRAN

Grand Lodge of AF&AM (in exile)
P.O. Box 25017, Los Angeles, CA 90025, USA

IRELAND

Grand Lodge of Ireland
17 Molesworth Street, Dublin 2
www.irish-freemasons.org

ISRAEL

Grand Lodge of the State of Israel
P.O. Box 33206, Tel Aviv 61331
www.freemasonry.org.il

ITALY

Grand Orient of Italy
Villa il Vascello, Via San Pancrazio 8, 00152 Rome
www.grandeoriente.it
Regular Grand Lodge of Italy
Lungotevere dei Mellini 17, 00193 Rome
www.grandlodge-italy.org
Grand Lodge of Italy
Via San Nicola de' Cesarini, 3 Area Sacra di Torre Argentina 00186 Rome
www.granloggia.it
Serenissima Grand Lodge
Palazzo del Sacramento, Piazza del Gesù,
www.serenissimagranloggia.it

Women's Grand Lodge of Italy
See website for contact details:
www.granloggiafemminile.it

IVORY COAST

Grand Lodge of Ivory Coast
08 B.P. 2028 Abidjan 08

JAPAN

Grand Lodge of Japan
1-3 Shibakoen, 4-Chome Minato-ku, Tokyo 105-0011
www.japan-freemasons.org

LATVIA

Grand Lodge of Latvia
See website for contact details:
www.masonicum.lv

LITHUANIA

Grand Lodge of AF&AM
See website for contact details:
www.freemasonry.lt

LUXEMBOURG

Grand Lodge of Luxembourg
B.P. 851, L-2018 Luxembourg
Grand Orient of Luxembourg
B.P. 3236, L-1021 Luxembourg
www.gol.lu

MEXICO
As for the US, there is a Grand Lodge for every state in Mexico.

Grand Lodge of 'Baja California'
Av. Revolucion No. 1651–3, Zona Centro C.P. 22000, Tijuana
Grand Lodge 'Benito Juarez' of Coahuila
Boulevard Constitucion 311 Pte. Ap. Post. 87 y 187, Torreon, C.P. 27000
Grand Lodge of Chiapas
Av. Central Norte y 5a. Calle Pte. No. 1, Ap. Post. No. 67, 30700 De Tapachula
Grand Lodge 'Cosmos' of Chihuahua
C/ Libertad No. 1004, Chihuahua, C.P. 31000
Grand Lodge of the Pacific
Guadalupe Victoria No. 39 Col. San Benito, Ap. Post. No. 5-118
Grand Lodge of Soberana
Manuel José Othon 335, Ap. Post. No. 104, San Luis Potosi, C.P. 78000
Grand Lodge of Nuevo Leon
Gral. Mariano Escobedo No. 414 Nte., Ap. Post. No. 309, C.P. 64000 Monterrey

Grand Lodge 'Occidental Mexicana'
  Lopez Cotilla No. 111 Zona Centro
  Guadalajara, JAL
Grand Lodge of Sinaloa
  Augurio No. 3410, Col. 4 de Marzo
  Culiacan, Sinaloa, C.P. 80020
Grand Lodge of Tamaulipas
  Encino No. 100, Colonia Aguila,
  Tampico, C.P. 89230
Grand Lodge 'Unida Mexicana'
  Benito Juarez No. 59, Ap. Post. 56,
  C.P. 91700 Veracruz
Grand Lodge Valle de Mexico
  Sadi Carnot No. 75, Col. San Rafael
  Delagacion Cuauhtemoc, C.P. 06470,
  Mexico D.F.
York Grand Lodge of Mexico
  Hegel No. 416, Polanco, C.P. 11560,
  Mexico, D. F.
  www.yorkrite.com/yglmx

MOROCCO

Grand Lodge 'El Andalous'
  11 rue Dayet Erroumi, appt 8,
  Agdal Rabat

THE NETHERLANDS

Great East of the Netherlands
  Prinsessegracht 27, 2514 AP
  The Hague
  www.vrijmetselarij.nl
Grand Lodge of Co-Masonry
  Wilhelminalaan 26, 3051 JS Rotterdam
  www.nggv.nl

NEW ZEALAND

Grand Lodge of AF&AM
  39–41 Ghuznee Street, Wellington 6035
  www.freemasons.co.nz

NICARAGUA

Symbolic Grand Lodge
  Edificio Armando Guido 1 cuadra al sur,
  2 al occidente, Managua
  www.geocities.com/gran_logia_
  de_nicaragua

NORWAY

Norwegian Order of Freemasons
  Nedre Vollgate 19, 0158 Oslo
  www.frimurer.no

PANAMA

Grand Lodge of Panama
  C/ 13, Final, Santa Ana, Panamá
  www.granlogiadepanama.org

PARAGUAY

Symbolic Grand Lodge of Paraguay
  P.O. Box 1178, C.P. 1209, Asunción
  www.masoneriaparaguaya.org.py

PERU

Grand Lodge of Peru
  Ave. José Galvez Barrenecheaa
  No. 599, San Isidro, Lima-27
  www.granlogiamasonesperu.org

PHILIPPINES

Grand Lodge of F&AM
  P. O. Box 990 Ermita, Manila
  www.glphils.org

POLAND

Grand Lodge of Poland
  Box 94, 00-950 Warsaw
  www.wlnp.pl

PORTUGAL

Legal Grand Lodge
  Rua João Saraiva, 34-1, 1700-250 Lisbon
  www.gllp.pt
National Grand Lodge
  Praça 5 de Outubro, 5370 Mirandela
  www.glnp.pt
Regular Grand Lodge of Portugal
  Rua Tenente Espanca, 17A, Moradia E,
  1050-220 Lisbon
  www.glrp.com.pt

ROMANIA

National Grand Lodge
  Sala Palatului - Ion Campineanu Str.
  Nr. 28, Et. 2, Sect.1 - 78664 Bucharest
  www.mlnr.ro

RUSSIA

Grand Lodge of Russia
  PO Box 2053, Moscow 101000
  www.freemasonry.ru

SCOTLAND

Grand Lodge of AF&AM
  Freemasons' Hall, 96 George Street
  Edinburgh EH2 3DH
  www.grandlodgescotland.com

SENEGAL

Grand Lodge of Senegal
  B.P. 442, Dakar, West Africa

SERBIA AND MONTENEGRO

Grand Lodge
  Staro sajmiste 20,11070 Novi Beograd

SOUTH AFRICA

Grand Lodge of AF&AM
  P.O. Box 46203, Orange Grove,
  Code 2119, Johannesburg
  www.grandlodge.co.za

SPAIN

Symbolic Grand Lodge of Spain
  Avinyó, 27, Barcelona
  www.glse.org
Grand Lodge of Spain
  Gran Via de les Corts Catalanes, 617,
  08007 Barcelona
  www.gle.es

SWEDEN

Swedish Order of Freemasons
  Blasieholmsgatan 6, 111 48 Stockholm
  www.frimurarorden.se

SWITZERLAND

Grand Lodge Alpina
  Rue du Petit-Beaulieu 1,
  CH-1004 Lausanne
  www.freimaurerei.ch
Grand Orient of Switzerland
  Case postale 94, CH-1073 Savigny
  www.g-o-s.ch
Mixed Grand Lodge
  See website for contact details:
  www.masonic.ch/GLMS
Women's Grand Lodge
  Case postale 278, CH-1211
  Le Lignon/Geneva
  www.glfs-masonic.ch

TOGO

National Grand Lodge
  P.O. Box 1103, Lome, West Africa

TURKEY

Grand Lodge of Turkey F&AM
  Nuruziya Sukak 25, 80050 Beyoglu,
  Istanbul
  www.mason.org.tr
Liberal Grand Lodge
  See website for contact details:
  www.mason-mahfili.org.tr

UNITED STATES
The United States has one Grand Lodge for
each state. In addition, there is a Prince Hall
Grand Lodge for most states: see the Prince
Hall Massachusetts website for links:
www.princehall.org

Alabama
  3033 Vaughn Rd., Montgomery
  36106-2731
  www.alagl.org
Alaska
  PO Box 190668, Anchorage 99519-0668
  www.alaska-mason.org
Arizona
  345 W. Monroe, Phoenix 85003-1684
  www.azmasons.org
Arkansas
  700 Scott St., Little Rock 72201-4693
  www.arkmason.com
California
  1111 California St., San Francisco
  94108-2284
  www.freemason.org
Colorado
  1130 Panorama, Colorado Springs
  80904-1798
  www.coloradomasons.org
Connecticut
  Masonic Home, Masonic Ave.,
  Wallingford 06492
  www.ctfreemasons.net
Delaware
  818 Market St., Wilmington
  19801-3011
  www.masonsindelaware.org
District of Columbia
  5428 MacArthur Blvd. NW,
  Washington, D.C. 20016-2541
  www.dcgrandlodge.org
Florida
  220 Ocean St., Jacksonville
  32202-3218
  www.glflamason.org
Georgia
  811 Mulberry, Macon 31298-5099
  www.glofga.org
Hawaii
  1270 Queen Emma St., Suite 612
  Honolulu
  www.hawaiifreemason.org
Idaho
  219 North 17th Street,
  Boise 83702-5187
  www.idahoaf.am
Illinois
  2866 Via Verde Street,
  Springfield 62703-4325
  www.ilmason.org
Indiana
  525 N. Illinois St., Indianapolis 46204
  www.indianamasons.org

Iowa
813 1st Ave. SE, Cedar Rapids
52401-5001
www.gl-iowa.org
Kansas
320 W. 8th St., Topeka 66601
www.gl-ks.org
Kentucky
300 Masonic Home Drive,
Masonic Home 40041
www.grandlodgeofkentucky.org
Louisiana
5800 Masonic Drive, Alexandria, 71301
www.la-mason.com/gl.htm
Maine
415 Congress St., Portland
04101-3500
www.mainemason.org
Maryland
304 International Circle,
Cockeysville 21030
www.mdmasons.org
Massachusetts
186 Tremont St., Boston 02111-1095
www.glmasons-mass.org
Michigan
233 E. Fulton, Grand Rapids
49503-3270
www.gl-mi.org
Minnesota
200 E. Plato Blvd., St. Paul
55107-1685
www.mn-mason.org
Mississippi
2400 23rd Ave., Meridian 39305
www.msgrandlodge.org
Missouri
6033 Masonic Drive, Suite B Columbia,
65202-6535
www.momason.org
Montana
425 N. Park, Helena 59624
www.grandlodgemontana.org
Nebraska
1240 N. 10th St., Lincoln 68508
www.nebraska-grand-lodge.org
Nevada
40 W. 1st St., Rm. 317,
Reno 89501-1424
www.nvmasons.org

New Hampshire
813 Beech St., Manchester
03104-3136
www.nhgrandlodge.org
New Jersey
1114 Oxmead Road, Burlington
08016-4200
www.njfreemasonry.org
New Mexico
1638 University N.E.,
Albuquerque 87125
www.nmmasons.org
New York
71 W. 23rd St., New York 010010-4149
www.nymasons.org
North Carolina
2921 Glenwood Ave., Raleigh
27608-1009
www.grandlodge-nc.org
North Dakota
201 14th Ave. N., Fargo 58102
www.glnd.org
Ohio
634 High St., Worthington
43085-0629
www.freemason.com
Oklahoma
102 S. Broad, Guthrie 73044
www.gloklahoma.org
Oregon
2150 Masonic Way, Forest Grove 97116
www.masonic-oregon.com
Pennsylvania
1 North Broad St., Philadelphia
19107-2598
www.pagrandlodge.org
Puerto Rico
PO Box 8385, Santurce 00910
Rhode Island
222 Taunton Ave, East Providence
02914-4556
www.rimasons.org
South Carolina
1445 Pisgah Church Rd, Lexington
29072-8937
www.scgrandlodgeafm.org
South Dakota
520 S. 1st Ave., Sioux Falls 57014-6902
www.mastermason.com/
southdakota

Tennessee
100 7th Ave. N., Nashville 37203
www.grandlodge-tn.org
Texas
715 Columbus, Waco 76701
www.grandlodgeoftexas.org
Utah
650 East South Temple St.,
Salt Lake City 84102-1141
www.utahgrandlodge.org
Vermont
49 East Road, Berlin, Barre,
05641-5390
www.vtfreemasons.org
Virginia
4115 Nine Mile Rd., Richmond
23223-4926
www.grandlodgeofvirginia.org
Washington
47 St. Helens Ave., Tacoma 98402-2698
www.freemason-wa.org
West Virginia
PO Box 2346, Charleston 25328-2346
www.wvmasons.org
Wisconsin
36275 Sunset Dr., Dousman 53118-9349
www.wisc-freemasonry.org
Wyoming
2125 Cy Avenue, Casper 82602
www.wyomingmasons.com

Other organizations in the US

Ancient and Accepted Scottish Rite
There are two jurisdictions in the US:

Southern Jurisdiction
The Supreme Council, 33°
1733 16th St. NW
Washington, D.C. 20009-3103
www.srmason-sj.org

Northen Jurisdiction
The Supreme Council, 33°
P.O. Box 519
Lexington, MA 02420-0519
www.supremecouncil.org

The York Rite
The York Rite is composed of three bodies:

General Grand Chapter
General Offices
P.O. Box 489, Danville,
KY 40423-0489
www.yorkrite.com/chapter

General Grand Council
General Offices
541 Crestview Drive, PO Box 310
Sherrard IL 61281
www.yorkrite.com/council

Grand Encampment of Knights Templar
5097 North Elston Avenue,
Suite 101, Chicago,
IL 60630-2460
www.knightstemplar.org

Ancient Arabic Order of the Nobles of the Mystic Shrine ('Shriners')
International Headquarters
2900 Rocky Point Dr., Tampa,
FL 33607-1460
www.shrinershq.org

Mystic Order, Veiled Prophets of the Enchanted Realm ('Grotto')
Supreme Council Office
1696 Brice Rd, Reynoldsburg,
OH 43068
www.scgrotto.com

Order of the Eastern Star
General Grand Chapter
1618 New Hampshire Avenue NW
Washington, DC 20009-2549
www.easternstar.org

URUGUAY

Grand Lodge of Uruguay
11300 Montevideo
www.masoneria-uruguay.org

VENEZUELA

Grand Lodge of Venezuela
Apartado de Correos No. 927
Carmelitas, Caracas 1010A
www.glrbv.org.ve

MASONIC MUSEUMS AND LIBRARIES

There are many Masonic museums and libraries around the world, almost all of which are freely open to the public. Here are some of the more interesting collections. Most have very informative and well-illustrated websites.

Austria

Rosenau Masonic Museum
A-3924 Schloß Rosenau 1, nr Zwettl
www.freimaurermuseum.at
Situated in Schloß Rosenau, this museum traces the history of Freemasonry in Austria, looking at such prominent members as Mozart. There is a small entrance charge.

Belgium

Belgian Museum of Freemasonry
rue de Laeken, 79, 1000 Brussels
www.mason.be/en/mus
Houses an important collection of Masonic objects, documents and books from the 18th century to the present day, and aims to show Freemasonry in an objective way as well as explaining the Masonic method.

Brazil

The Grand Orient of São Paulo has an interesting virtual museum:
www.gosp.org.br/museu

England

Library and Museum of Freemasonry
Freemasons' Hall, 60 Great
Queen St, London WC2B 5AZ
www.freemasonry.london.museum
One of the largest collections in the world, covering the history of Freemasonry from the foundation of the premier Grand Lodge in 1717 to the present day. Has extensive collections of objects relating to Friendly Societies. There is also an excellent Library. Admission is free.

Germany

German Masonic Museum, Bayreuth
Im Hofgarten 1, 95444 Bayreuth
www.freimaurer.org/museum
Collecting began as a private museum

founded in 1902, attached to the Lodge 'Eleusis zur Verschwiegenheit', No. 6, founded in 1741 and one of the oldest Lodges in Germany. Since then it has grown into one of the largest collections of Masonic material in the world. The Lodge building is illustrated on p. 136.

France

Museum of the Grand Orient of France
16, rue Cadet, 75009 Paris
www.godf.org/musee.asp
Founded in 1889, this is an important and diverse collection including prints, Meissen figurines, and Voltaire's apron.

Museum of the French National Grand Loge
rue Christine de Pisan, 12, 75017 Paris
www.grandelogenationalefrancaise.com
A grand range of material on the history of French Freemasonry.

Museum of the Grand Lodge of France
8, rue de puteaux, 75017 Paris
www.gldf.org
Contains a collection of around 2,000 objects.

Ireland

Grand Lodge Library and Museum
Freemason's Hall, 17 Molesworth St.
Dublin 2
www.irish-freemasons.org
An excellent collection of Masonic objects relating to Freemasonry in Ireland. Information about the Museum is available on the website.

Netherlands

'Prins Frederick' Masonic Cultural Centre
Jan Evertstraat 9 te Den Haag
www.vrijmetselarij.nl
This collection covers the 250-year history of Freemasonry in the Netherlands, and also includes a library.

Norway

Norwegian Order of Freemasons Museum
Address as for Grand Lodge
www.frimurer.no/nettutstilling.htm

Scotland

Grand Lodge of Scotland Museum of Freemasonry
96 George Street, Edinburgh, EH2 3DH
www.grandlodgescotland.com/glos/museum
This collection exists to 'inform and display the 400 years of Scottish Freemasonry', and includes the oldest Lodge Minutes in the world, dating to 1599.

Turkey

Masonic Museum
See website for details:
www.masonmuzesi.org

United States

Most Grand Lodges have good-sized libraries of Masonic publications, many of which are open to the public – see the previous pages for contact details. It is also worth consulting the website of the Masonic Libraries and Museums Assocation – www.mlmassn.org – for more information.

Livingston Masonic Library
71 W 23rd Street, New York 10010-4171
www.nymasoniclibrary.org
Holds over 60,000 volumes detailing Masonic history and philosophy. Also has extensive collections of Masonic art, memorabilia, ritual artifacts and jewelry.

George Washington Masonic National Memorial
101 Callahan Drive
Alexandria, Virginia 22301
www.gwmemorial.org
This distinctive and impressive building houses a large collection of historical artifacts (including objects belonging to Washington) as well as displays explaining the various Higher Degrees in the United States. Open daily, free admission.

Minnesota Masonic Museum
11501 Masonic Home Drive
Bloomington, 55437-3699
www.minnesotamasonicmuseum.org

National Heritage Museum
33 Marrett Road, Lexington, MA 02421
www.nationalheritagemuseum.org
A collection supported by the Scottish Rite, N.J., on American history, with substantial

Masonic holdings. It also hosts temporary exhibitions and contains a large library of Masonic material. Free admission.

Phoenix Masonry Masonic Museum
A virtual museum with a large range of material organized into categories.
www.phoenixmasonry.org/masonicmuseum

Library and Museum of the Supreme Council 33°, S.J.
House of the Temple, 1733 Sixteenth Street, NW, Washington, D.C. 20009-3103
www.srmason-sj.org/library.htm
Various collections, including the Albert Pike Museum, the Americanism Museum, and impressive international holdings.

Grand Lodge of Ohio Museum
634 High St., Worthington
www.ohglmuseum.com
Open by appointment only.

Masonic Library and Museum of Pennsylvania
Masonic Temple, 1 North Broad Street
Philadelphia, PA 19107
www.pagrandlodge.org/mlam
Founded in 1908, this includes much material relating to Masonic Presidents, including the apron presented to George Washington by Lafayette.

Allen E. Roberts Masonic Library and Museum
4115 Nine Mile Road, Richmond, Virginia 23223-4926
www.grandlodgeofvirginia.org/library1.htm

Masonic Library and Museum
Grand Lodge of Iowa, A.F.& A. M
PO Box 279, Cedar Rapids, 52406-0279
showcase.netins.net/web/iowamasons/library.html
One of the best collections of Masonic material in the United States. The library is particularly good.

Institute for Masonic Studies
California Grand Lodge, 1111 California Street, San Francisco, CA 994108-2282
www.freemason.org

A huge amount has been published on Freemasonry over the past three hundred years; here we offer a sample of the more useful publications.

General

Carr, H., *The Freemason at Work*, London, 1976
Provides answers about the history, ritual and symbolism of Freemasonry.

Coil, H. W., *Masonic Encyclopedia*, Richmond, VA, 1996
Deals with almost every aspect of Freemasonry, in a pragmatic rather than mystical way. Written in 1961, it has remained in print since, and updated. It is among the most useful sources of factual material about the Order.

Duriegl, G., with S. Winkler, *Freimaurer*, Vienna, 1992
A beautifully illustrated German book providing a detailed description of Freemasonry in Germany.

Hamill, J., *The History of English Freemasonry*, Hinckley, 1994
An authoritative analysis of the origins, history, and practice of English Freemasonry, including overseas.

——, and R. Gilbert (eds), *Freemasonry, a Celebration of the Craft*, London, 1999
This deals with the origins, history and basic teachings of Freemasonry, and cites many famous people who have been Masons. Excellent authority.

Hoyos, A. de (ed.), *Freemasonry in Context*, Lexington, 2004
A reliable collection of articles from the Scottish Rite research publication, *Heredom*. Three general subjects are covered: history, ritual and controversy. Forward by Dr Steven C. Bullock.

Jones, B. E., *Freemasons' Guide and Compendium*, Orpington, 2003
This was published to provide a means of self-education for Masons.

Chapter 1

Campbell, J., *Hero with a Thousand Faces*, Princeton, 2004
An analysis of Classical mythology that suggests they tell the story of human interior growth. It is the story of the mystical ascent that was the essence of the Renaissance.

Churton, T., *The Golden Builders*, Weiser, 2005
A serious study of the philosophical essence of the Renaissance from which the first Masonic activity emerged. It is a valuable work providing a background which is rarely acknowledged and understood today.

Naudon, P., *The Secret History of Freemasonry*, Inner Traditions, 2005
The author is a French legal expert and Freemason who examines Freemasonry's alleged connection to the Knights Templar, primitive and medieval building societies.

Stevenson, D., *The First Freemasons*, MacMillan, 1989

——, *The Origins of Freemasonry*, Cambridge, 1990
Serious academic works which outlines the apparent incorporation of Scottish Gentlemen into operative Masonic Lodges in Scotland.

Yates, F. A., *The Occult Philosophy in the Elizabethan Age*, London, 1979
Historical analysis of the history of thought in the Renaissance period, which develops the hypothesis of the 'Hermetic/Cabbalistic tradition'.

——, *The Rosicrucian Enlightenment*, London, 1999
The best analysis of the three Rosicrucian documents, and speaks of their content and implications, as well as their relationship with Freemasonry.

Chapter 2

Anderson, J., *Constitutions*, Kessinger Pub. Co., 2003
The first Constitutions of Freemasonry, written by James Anderson and adopted by the premier Grand Lodge in 1723 are available with a useful introduction. They give an insight into the attitudes of Masons in the early period of the Order.

Bailey, F., *The Spirit of Masonry*, London, 1957
This book sets out an understanding of the Craft that is oriented toward interior work and the mystical ascent.

Carr, H., *Early French Exposures*, London, 1971
A compilation of various 18th-century French publications on Masonry. Provides interesting insight into anti-Masonic thought.

Hamilton, J. D., *Material Culture of the American Freemasons*, Lexington, 1994
An illustrated book on the material held in the Museum of Our National Heritage, Lexington, Mass. It explains the Masonic artifacts in a working context.

Jackson, A.C.F., *English Masonic Exposures*, London, 1986

Knoop, D., G. Jones, D. Hamer, *The Early Masonic Catechisms*, London, 1975
A collection of early documents, mostly exposures, alleging to describe the early Masonic workings. The text of the material may be unreliable, but the work of identifying it and organizing the documents is very well done.

——, *Early Masonic Pamphlets*, London, 1945
A collection of Masonic pamphlets, newspaper articles and advertisements printed between 1638 and 1735. Carefully done.

Mackey, A., *The History of Freemasonry*, Gramercy, 2005
Mackey, a prominent Freemason who died in 1881, discusses various legends and hypotheses about Masonic origins.

Wesley, C. H., *Prince Hall, Life and Legacy*, 1977
This book gives a good summary of Prince Hall's work in establishing African-American Freemasonry.

Chapter 3

Beresniak, B., *Symbols of Freemasonry*, 1997
This is an illustrated book originally published in France. It is organized by type of object.

Dyer, C., *Symbolism in Craft Freemasonry*, Hinckley, 1991
Dyer discusses the meaning and symbolic interpretation of the objects used in the Craft Degrees. Very useful.

——, *William Preston and His Work*, Hinckley, 2002
Preston was very influential in the 'standardization' of the Degrees and their meaning.

Horne, A., *Sources of Masonic Symbolism*, Richmond, 1981
Seeks to identify the sources of the symbols, a difficult task because of the lack of early evidence. A useful work that aims at objectivity.

——, *King Solomon's Temple in the Masonic Tradition*, Wellingborough, 1972

Hoyos, A. de (ed.), *Symbolism of the Blue Degrees of Freemasonry, Albert Pike's Esoterika*, Washington, D.C., 2005
A collection of essays by Pike that describe his understanding of the Craft Degrees, focusing on interior work.

MacNulty, W. K., *The Way of the Craftsman*, London, 2002
This book starts with an analysis of the Renaissance. Then it presents the Degrees of Craft Masonry as a model of the psyche; and, in the context of the Hermetic/Cabbalistic tradition, it suggests an approach for using the teachings of the Degrees as a guide for the mystical ascent.

——, *Freemasonry, a Journey through Ritual and Symbol*, London, 2005
A summarized version of the title above, with the benefit of some beautiful art.

Wilmshurst, W. L., *The Meaning of Masonry*, Gramercy, 1995
This work outlines the Craft Degrees of

Freemasonry as a philosophy and as a philosophical method of self-realization. It also touches upon the Holy Royal Arch. Deeply valuable.

——, *The Masonic Initiation*, Kessinger, 2004
Freemasonry is commonly called a 'system of morality'. In this work, Wilmshurst expands on that idea, pointing out that the Order is a Science and an Art. The science is presented as the work of understanding one's situation; the art is presented as the work of purifying one's self and living the life envisioned by one's Faith.

Chapter 4

Fox, W. L. (ed.), *Valley of the Craftsman*, Lexington, 2001
A pictorial history of the American Scottish Rite, Southern Jurisdiction, covering the period 1801 to 2001.

——, *Lodge of the Double-headed Eagle*, Univ. of Arkansas, 1997
This is a serious, detailed and authoritative history of The Ancient and Accepted Scottish Rite, Southern Jurisdiction, in the United States. It starts with the formation of the Supreme Council in Charleston, NC, in 1801 and provides an insight into the influence of the Scottish Rite in the development of America's democratic, civic and moral values.

Hinman, E., R. Denslow, C. Hunt, *A History of the Cryptic Rite*, 2 vols, General Grand Council Royal and Select Masters, USA, 1918

Hutchens, R. R., *A Bridge to Light*, Anderson, 1992
In this work Hutchens presents his interpretation of the Scottish Rite Degrees 4–32. They are his understandings and, like Pike's, they are not presented as absolute facts. The work provides an interesting insight into the Scottish Rite, and is significantly easier to read than *Morals and Dogma*.

Mandleberg, J., *Ancient and Accepted, a chronicle of proceedings 1845–1945 of the Supreme Council established in England in 1845*, Supreme Council for England and Wales, 1995

Miner, S. W., *Let Your Work Become Your Mark*, Highland Springs, VA., 1986
Miner is a Past Grand Master of the Grand Lodge of Virginia and the Past Grand Secretary of the Grand Lodge of the District of Columbia. In this collection of essays he describes how one can apply the principles of the Royal Arch, particularly the Mark Degrees, to one's life and actions.

Pike, A., *Morals and Dogma*, Kessinger, 2004
Albert Pike was the Grand Commander of

the Scottish Rite, Southern Jurisdiction from 1859–91. He was responsible for the successful organization and growth of that Order. This work is a collection of essays, one for each of the thirty-two Degrees.

Turnbull, E. V., R. Denslow, *A History of Royal Arch Masonry*, 3 vols., General Grand Chapter Royal Arch Masons, USA, 1956

Chapter 5
Bullock, S. C., *Revolutionary Brotherhood*, Univ. of North Carolina, 1996
Bullock traces the history of Freemasonry from its English origins through its first hundred years in America. He analyses its key role in the development of early American ideals such as liberty and equality. He sees the Order as a significant influence in the socio-cultural transition from the colony of a monarchy to Jacksonian democracy.

Grosjean, M. (Preface), *Le Droit Humain*
An outline of the origins and development of the Order of International Co-Freemasonry, 'Le Droit Humain'.

Hoyos, A. de, S. B. Morris, *Is It True What They Say About Freemasonry?*, 2004
In recent years detractors of Freemasonry have gone beyond their practice of making critical statements, and they have invented vicious lies about the Order. This book identifies several of these fabrications and exposes them for what they are.

Piatigorsky, A., *Who's Afraid of Freemasons?*, London, 1997
Piatigorsky is a professor of comparative religion. In this work he deals with the history of Freemasonry, an analysis of the ritual and symbolism, and a sociological analysis of Freemasonry's critics.

Chapter 6
Haggard, F. D., *The Clergy and the Craft*, Missouri Lodge of Research, 1970
Haggard is a well-known US Protestant minister and Freemason.

Hannah, W., *Darkness Visible*, St Augustine Press, 1998
Rev. Walton Hannah, at first a clergyman in the Church of England, later a Catholic Priest, first published this work in 1952. He understands, incorrectly, Freemasonry to be a religion; and in that context he considers membership in it to be incompatible with the duties of a Christian. Sadly, his work is based on a misunderstanding of the Order, but one must acknowledge that this is among the most thoughtful, and the least vitriolic of anti-Masonic publications.

Ovason, D., *The Secret Architecture of our Nation's Capital: The Masons and the Building of Washington, D.C.*, New York, 2000

——, *The Secret Symbols of the Dollar Bill*, New York, 2000

Chapter 7
Denslow, W. R., *10,000 Famous Freemasons*, 4 vols. Richmond, VA, 1957
Foreword by Harry S. Truman, P.G.M.

Haywood, H. L., *Famous Masons*, Richmond, VA, 1944

Tabbert, M. A., *American Freemasons*, New York, 2005
Tabbert outlines the history of Order; but most of the work is about the interaction of Freemasonry with American society, the principles that are to be applied and the prominent American Masons who have contributed to the American communities.

OTHER USEFUL RESOURCES

Websites
There are many websites dedicated to Freemasonry. The following are particularly long-established, interesting and helpful.

www.bessel.org
Has a huge amount of information and statistics on Freemasonry around the world.

internet.lodge.org.uk
A UGLE-recognized Lodge (No. 9659) on the Internet, with members from around the world.

www.freemasonry.org
The 'Philathenes Web Portal', a springboard to other Masonic websites. Also has many essays on a variety of topics.

www.freemasonry.bcy.ca/info.html
One of the best websites on Freemasonry, attractive, easy to use, and packed full of information and useful links. Scholarly.

www.masonicinfo.com
A solid site with some great (and often very amusing) pages on anti-Masonry.

web.mit.edu/dryfoo/Masonry
'The World's Oldest Masonic Web-Site', according to the creator. Another good source of information.

www.freemasonrywatch.org
For good measure, an anti-Masonic website, with plenty of conspiracy theories.

Masonic Research
There are dozens of Masonic research groups around the world – the following are well-established and have a good web presence.

Canonbury Masonic Research Centre
www.canonbury.ac.uk
An important centre of Masonic research, that also hosts regular lectures.

Sheffield University Centre for Masonic Research
www.freemasonry.dept.shef.ac.uk
Contains out-of-date texts for rituals, which make fascinating reading.

The Cornerstone Society
www.cornerstonesociety.com

The Philalethes Society
www.freemasonry.org/psoc

Quatuor Coronati Lodge of Research
www.quatuorcoronati.com
The oldest Lodge of Research in the world, which also runs a correspondence circle. Publishes *Ars Quatuor Coronati Lodge Transactions*, a scholarly journal on Masonic history and practice.

Scottish Rite Research Society
www.srmason-sj.org/web/srrs.htm
Publishes *Heredom* (see below)

Magazines and Journals
Almost every jurisdiction has its own magazine or periodical – copies can often be obtained by contacting the relevant Grand Lodge. These are some that cut across jurisdictions:

Freemasonry Today
www.freemasonrytoday.com

Masonic Magazine
www.masonicmagazine.com

Renaissance Traditionnelle
www.renaissance-traditionnelle.org
Perhaps the best philosophical French Masonic journal, with some articles in English.

Heredom
www.srmason-sj.org/web/heredom.htm
The journal of the Scottish Rite Research Society. Has some articles on-line.

Pietre-Stones Review of Freemasonry
www.freemasons-freemasonry.com
An online review with a wealth of articles and essays.

Illustrations are listed by page number.
a above; *b* below; *l* left; *r* right; *c* centre

Abbreviations
BNF   Bibliothèque nationale de France
LOC   Library of Congress, Washington, D.C.
PC   Photograph by Painton Cowen

ACKNOWLEDGMENTS

The following people have offered their help and knowledge in putting this book together: Alan W. Adkins, Donald L. Albert, Tim S. Anderson, Yasha Beresiner, Richard Curtis, Arturo de Hoyos (Grand Archivist and Grand Historian Supreme Council, 33°, Southern Jurisdiction, USA), Geir Gramvik, John Hamill, Georgia Hershfeld, Jurn Kerkkamp, Eliane Kesteloot (Women's Grand Lodge of Belgium), Ken McCarty, William R. Kruger, Barry Lyons, S. Brent Morris, Thad Peterson (Deutsches Freimaurermuseum, Bayreuth), Marcel de Prins, Brian Roberts (Grand Commander, 'Le Droit Humain', England), Thomas Savini (Chancellor Robert R. Livingston Masonic Library of Grand Lodge, New York), Gilbert Savitski, George D. Seghers and Mark Tabbert

I should like to thank in particular everybody at the Library and Museum of Freemasonry at the United Grand Lodge of England, London, for their kind assistance. In particular I owe a great debt to the Director, Diane Clements, for her support and for allowing photography of the items in her charge; to the Curator, Mark Dennis, the Assistant Curator, Andrew Tucker, and Cataloguer, Alison Royle, whose knowledge and expertise greatly benefited the book; and to Martin Cherry, the Librarian, whose knowledge of the archives produced some wonderful material. I am also grateful to Painton Cowen, who expertly photographed so many of the splendid works in this book.

Finally, I should like to thank everybody at Thames & Hudson, in particular Christopher Dell, Karin Fremer, Susanna Friedman and Alessandra Sauven.